Inspiring Leadership

A Guide to Mastering Leadership, Business Management, Organization, Development and Building High Performance Teams

GW00492660

© **Copyright 2019 - Peter Allen. All rights reserved.**

The contents of this book may not be reproduced, duplicated or transmitted without direct written permission from the author.

Under no circumstances will any legal responsibility or blame be held against the publisher for any reparation, damages, or monetary loss due to the information herein, either directly or indirectly.

Legal Notice:

You cannot amend, distribute, sell, use, quote or paraphrase any part or the content within this book without the consent of the author.

Disclaimer Notice:

Please note the information contained within this document is for educational and entertainment purposes only. No warranties of any kind are expressed or implied. Readers acknowledge that the author is not engaging in the rendering of legal, financial, medical or professional advice. Please consult a licensed professional before attempting any techniques outlined in this book.

By reading this document, the reader agrees that under no circumstances are is the author responsible for any losses, direct or indirect, which are incurred as a result of the use of information contained within this document, including, but not limited to, — errors, omissions, or inaccuracies.

Table of Contents

Chapter Six: Leadership Behaviors, Development of Leadership Style and Skills

Chapter 7 How Great Leaders Inspire Action/ The 7 Great Leadership Traits

Conclusion

References

Introduction

Thank you for buying this book. I hope you find it informative and useful.

The world is changing rapidly, and the competition is rising day by day. The corporate world has become one of the most challenging and essential employment fields today. The relationship between employees and the employer are being studied in detail by many. One of the most important questions related to this world is leadership and leadership skills.

Being a good leader and possessing good leadership skills is essential. There are many different styles of leadership, and a lot of people are often confused about these styles. Many people believe their leadership style is the best, but with a lot of research, it has been proven that no one leadership style is the best. Each leadership style has its use. Thus, there exists no one right way to lead in all circumstances. So, how do you traverse this complex world of leadership and management? This book will serve as a guide for you to master leadership, organization, and business management. It will also teach you how to build and develop high-performance teams and how to manage them.

There is a myth that leadership needs to be innate, and you cannot learn leadership skills. This is absolutely false. You can learn leadership skills, and also improve and develop your overall personality and attitude. You can learn to be a great leader by focusing on improving particular leadership skills. True leadership is a lifelong journey that requires constant learning and this book will help you on this journey by providing you various tips, tricks, and methods that will help you become a great and successful leader. Peter Allen, a well-renowned business leader, believes that leadership is a skill that can be acquired. While having innate talents can help you to become a good leader, they cannot make you a successful leader if you do not combine them with dedication, spirit, perseverance, and the thirst to learn. Many great leaders have admitted that they did not have any innate talent for leadership, but they still became successful because they persevered.

The corporate world is changing rapidly, and the things that were norms just a couple of years ago are now considered to be taboo. While the strength and passion of a leader are still considered to be assets, his or her lack of emotions is looked down upon. Now if the leader is not in touch with his or her emotions or does not care for his or her employees, then his or her chances of becoming successful become almost negligible. It is necessary to create a positive workplace culture and a positive personality and stick to it. You cannot be successful if you are not optimistic and positive. If you think that you are not earning success, then you should change the way you do business and change the way you lead your life as well. Changes often seem daunting but don't worry. This book contains various methods that will show you how changes are necessary and how they can be made without any risk. These changes are easy to adapt and can be incorporated into your corporate world with ease. You should also try to incorporate these changes into your personal world, as it will allow you to create a sustainable business. Having a sustainable business in the current world is necessary because it keeps on changing almost every day. Try to motivate your employees and create empowerment and engagement. Empowered employees will make your group strong and functional. You can empower employees by being an effective and inspirational leader. For instance, great leaders like Napoleon, Winston Churchill, Steve Jobs, Bill Gates, Joan of Arc, Angela Merkel etc. are or were considered to be successful leaders because they inspired their people. They are considered to be great leaders because they were able to guide their people through times of crisis. They supported creativity and innovation and used multiple methods to conquer their goals. At times, they changed their leadership styles so that they could incorporate other people into their groups. Thus, these leaders became great leaders because they were flexible, bold, and passionate.

This book will help you become a passionate, dedicated, inspiring, and successful leader as well. It will help you to develop your greatest potential as a leader. It will inspire action in you and will help you to inspire your team members as well. Remember, bad leadership has brought down not only groups and companies but even empires in the past. Bad leadership can ruin your fortune and can throw you out of the limelight. It is thus crucial to change your leadership style immediately! So, go on and read this book and change your life around!

Start now!

Chapter One: Dispelling Myths

Leadership is one of the most significant roles that a person can take on in their life. It is significant not only because of the perks and honor but also because of the duties and traits associated with it. Leadership is not an easy task. It is a prolonged process that takes time to develop. It can be confusing and frustrating at times. This is why a lot of myths are prevalent about leadership. These myths make leadership out to be a highly difficult and complex role. They also create an image that makes leadership seem to be a talent that only a few can possess. In this chapter, let us have a look at some of the most significant myths associated with leadership.

The Myth of Innate Leadership

The formation of fact/truth is a complex philosophical argument. Often when a statement is repeated enough times, people begin to accept it as a truth. Some of such statements include: "Elephants have really strong memories.", "Women are emotional and difficult to understand.", and the most common one being "Leaders cannot be made, they can only be born."

All of the above notions have been debunked except for the last one. The prevalence of the myth that 'Leaders are born and not made' is confusing. It is perhaps still prevalent due to gate-keeping practices. This stubborn notion is a myth that has hindered the growth of not only many individuals but also a lot of corporations. It is a prejudice that has led to a lot of problems. It stops the development of others as well as ourselves in attaining the title of great leader.

First things first, not everyone wants to be a leader. Not everyone believes leadership is an attractive position. They do not want to spend time becoming a leader. This is a valid opinion. But this does not mean that these people are not capable of leadership. Everyone can be a leader if they want to be. This is because leadership is a set of practices that can be learned through observation. Many people do not think that they can be a leader just because they have been fed this information since the beginning.

A lot of studies have been done on this topic of nature vs nurture. According to almost all researchers, there are certain 'natural' factors that can make us great leaders. For instance, the degree of intelligence, our social skills, innate empathy etc. According to some researchers, around 30% of our innate talents can help us turn into a great leader. The remaining 70% can only be learned through practice and observation. Your 30% innate talent will be useless if you do not learn how to use it and combine it with the remaining 70% of observation. Thus, nature and nurture are both equally responsible for creating a great leader.

People who genuinely believe that leaders are born and not made will always have a different point of view toward leadership. They will believe it to be a formal and autonomous position. People who believe that leaders are born will also believe in their authoritarian power. They will believe that a leader can only be successful if they follow the protocols of hierarchy. For them, formality makes the best and most successful leaders. Such people think that only rule-abiding leaders can be successful. In contrast to this, people who believe that leaders are not born and are rather made will always look at leadership as a collective and collaborative endeavor. For them, teams make leaders and not vice versa.

The beliefs related to 'made' and 'born' leaders also affect our selection of leaders. Teams who believe that leadership is an innate quality will always choose a person who seems to be a leader ignoring the later development a person may undergo. Expecting a person to be a great leader just because of a few innate qualities can prove harmful to the mental health of the individual and the strength of the company.

Thus, if you want to become a great leader or want to choose a great leader, then you should try to seek a balance between 'nature and nurture.'

Developing a leader is not a scientific activity; rather, it is an artistic endeavor. Like an artist, a leader should possess some sort of conceptual knowledge and innate skills. An artist can benefit a lot if he or she possesses these skills, but their art cannot progress if they do not practice it regularly. Similarly, a leader cannot become successful and grow in his or her field until he or she practices and learns from observation.

If you want to become a great leader, just focus on your surroundings and your work. Try to maintain cordial relationships with everyone. You need to learn how to observe things and how to utilize them for your own benefits. This will allow you to become a successful leader soon.

In the end, you should remember that anyone could excel at anything if they are dedicated and passionate about it. Leadership is a skill and not a genetic trait. Here is a quote to keep you inspired.

"Leaders aren't born; they are made. And they are made just like anything else, through hard work. And that's the price we'll have to pay to achieve that goal or any goal." - Vince Lombardi

Leadership is possessing powers over others

One of the biggest myths associated with leadership is that leaders are omnipotent. You cannot be a leader unless you possess power others and dominate them. This is an unfortunate myth that perpetuates the stereotype of a selfish and angry boss. This creates a negative atmosphere in the workplace, which leads to a lot of problems later. A company cannot progress unless a positive workplace atmosphere is maintained for which, the team and the team leader both need to understand their positions.

There have been a lot of selfish leaders who have only focused on their personal gains and development often while sacrificing others. It is said that power can corrupt even the best of people. This has been proven by many examples in the past; however, it is still a myth. Power does not corrupt people, rather the notions associated with power and the theories perpetuated about it, and corrupt people.

Leaders try to control their employees to get what they want. They like to dominate others to do their bidding. This kind of negative and narcissistic behaviour can ruin a company. Not all leaders act like this now. The notions and concept of leadership have undergone significant changes in the past few decades.

The pace of life and the level of competition has drastically changed in the modern world. Businesses, employees, and employers all have become action-oriented. People often believe that sometimes you need to sacrifice others for the greater good. Often the employees and team members become the 'sacrificial goats.'

Leaders who are disconnected from themselves and their team members continue to act in ways that can hider interpersonal connections. Leadership is not a struggle for power; rather, it is a nourishing and balancing endeavor. A leader not only needs to nourish his or her team members but also maintain a balance between their work and attitude.

A leader cannot be power-hungry, as it will destroy the harmony in the team. Dominance and respect are like yin and yang; you need both to control and guide people. Maintaining a balance between these two is crucial, or you will become an unpopular leader soon.

Static Leadership

Another aspect related to power-hungriness and leadership is the belief that leadership is static. Many people (including many leaders) believe that once a person becomes a leader, they continue to be a leader throughout their life. In reality, leadership is rarely this static; rather, it is dynamic, effective, and alive. It changes frequently.

Thus, everyone is a leader in away. You do not need to be in the front to lead people; you can also inspire and guide people from the back or even outside the team. You will find out more about this in the subsequent section.

Leaders are positively influential

People believe that leaders are heroic, smart, and intelligent. They believe that all leaders possess excellent problem-solving capabilities and that they can tackle even the most complex of problems and come up with solutions almost instantaneously. They believe that leaders can change the world for good on their own. This goes against all the collaborative and inclusive practices that leaders are supposed to undertake. This kind of reading of leaders is not only shallow but is quite one-dimensional as well.

It is true that leaders can be influential, but not all leaders are good. Many times, the solutions put forward by leaders are ineffective because they do not undergo rigorous and committed debate with the situation. Three things are essential if you want to become a great leader: Critical thinking, curiosity, and inclusiveness.

Leaders who can be a positive influence on others include leaders who understand their strengths and weaknesses. People who understand their own limitations know what their problems are, and they often work in the direction to solve or get rid of them. Leadership is a team sport. You cannot play it without collaborative efforts. Leaders understand that they need a diverse team to influence people. They understand that if they truly want to innovate, they will need to put a lot of efforts.

Everyone knows that great leaders are often great speakers. But not many people know that to be a great leader, you also need to be a great listener as well. Great leaders understand that their role in the team is to understand and inspire and not to answer others. They know that they are supposed to hire excellent people and get regular inputs from them. They understand their mistakes and allow others to correct them.

Leaders can inspire and empower others to become great leaders. Their ultimate goal is their best version. They should create a team that can work just as well, even if they are not present.

Tom Peters once said: "Leaders don't create more followers; they create more leaders." This quote shows how leaders can help the innate talents of people develop.

A negative aspect associated with leadership is that leaders do not like to fail. Failure is a crucial part of discovery and innovation. You cannot grow unless you fail. If you do not like to fail, you tend to stick to the old methods of the past. This hinders innovation and creativity. Leaders who like to stick to the past methods often force their employees to use the old methods as well. This creates a negative influence circle and stagnates the growth of the team. The elements of curiosity and exploration die in such situations just because the leader, and in turn, the team is not ready to try new things.

A person can only learn through failure and thus, it is the responsibility of the leader to embrace failure and help his team members to accept it as well.

Leaders entirely control group outcomes

A bad leader can ruin a good group, while a good leader can make a bad group excellent. It is true that a leader plays an important role in the functioning and progress of a group, but it does not mean that the leader is responsible for the outcomes of the team. Unlike the game of chess, a team does not lose when their leader exits. A team continues to survive even if their leader is changed.

Leaders often lead groups and teams. A leader is supposed to guide, control, and help the members of a group. A good/bad leader can really influence the outcome of a team, but he or she can rarely change it. A leader can be compared to a football coach. You may bring in the best coach in the world to coach a team, but you still cannot make the team win if they do not put efforts and dedication. A team can only succeed when all the members put in efforts and show spirit.

A team is a collaboration, and it can only succeed when it works in collaboration.

While it is true that a leader is expected to be the spokesperson of a group, but leadership is a varied construct that comes in many forms. Sometimes you do not even need to be in the team to lead it. True leaders are supposed to be humble, and this humbleness can only be achieved with communication and experience.

Hogging the limelight and usurping every opportunity to shine the brightest in a group can create a negative image of your group. Many popular leaders have always been out of the limelight and still have transformed industries.

A good leader is always able to control his or her ego. He or she looks for opportunities to benefit his or her company. This does not mean that they do not possess any ego or self-interest; rather, every leader in this world has an ego and has ambition. Without ambition, a person cannot become a leader. But good leaders channel their ambition in a way that benefits their industry/team. Thus, leaders possess a dualistic nature where they are often bold and humble, and willful yet modest.

It is always recommended to remember what Harry S. Truman said:

"You can accomplish anything in life, provided that you do not mind who gets the credit."

All groups have a designated leader

Once upon a time, people used to believe that all groups need a leader who can sit at the top and guide and control everything. This belief was still prevalent a few decades ago. But now the times have changed, and people have realized that the leader does not sit at the top of the 'power pyramid'. Now there are more than one leader in a group. In fact, nowadays, many groups do not have a designated leader at all.

Gone are the days when leaders were supposed to be all-powerful and smart demigods who would guide their teams through difficult situations. People now understand that leadership is a multidimensional project. Almost all members of a group move through various dimensions of leadership throughout the day. All of us are leaders in one-way or another. It is thus necessary to use every member's talent for the benefit of the team. A team is a collaborative effort and making leadership a collaborative effort can make a significantly positive change in the functioning of the group.

Gone are the days when the leader used to be the 'lone wolf' who would isolate himself or herself from the group to appear more dynamic, bold, and powerful. People used to believe that if the leader mingled with the team, he or she would not be able to retain the 'alpha' position as others would find out about his or her weaknesses and overall attitude. The myth of pomposity and authority would shatter, and he or she would no longer be a mystical and enigmatic figure.

Everyone has a weakness, but everyone also has strengths. Nowadays, people in a group concentrate on their strengths and try to use them to counter their weaknesses. This forms a nearly unbeatable group. Every member of the group is now a leader. Good leaders now are skillful and can evoke leadership qualities from others. They are generous and bold.

Group Members Resist Leaders and Change

The world is changing rapidly, and there is an exponential growth in the world of computers. Its impact is seen on almost all facets of life, including business and entrepreneurship. While change is happening everywhere, organizational change is still difficult and will need time to happen. But if these changes do not happen soon, the organizations will collapse. Leaders are often the harbinger of changes. There is a myth doing rounds that group members resist leaders who want to bring changes.

Many seniors too blame that the employees are not ready to accept the changes. At times this may be true, but mostly it is due to the gross misunderstanding of people and overestimation. Leaders need to look at things effectively if they want to bring changes and implement them effectively.

Leading requires a lot of people skills that not a lot of people possess.

Group members do not resist changes irrationally. Similarly, they do not resist leaders either. People rarely resist others if they can see that whatever the leader does will be in their best interests. Let us have a look at eight reasons due to which your group members may resist you.

Loss of status

Nobody likes to change if the change is going to harm our current situation. In administrative or organizational settings, this means that the managers, peers, employees, and even the leaders will resist change if the change means that their role will make their role obsolete. These people will believe that their leader is trying to harm them and will, therefore, resist him or her.

Changes are essential but changing it in a positive way is necessary. While it is possible to force change as a leader, you will soon find that this is not a long-term strategy. While it may show some positive results in the beginning, but in the long-term, it will end up causing more harm than benefits. If you overuse this method, you will ultimately harm your effectiveness and your employees will start to resist you.

Poorly aligned reward systems

The leaders get things that they reward. This means that the employees will show passion and dedication only if they are rewarded well. People will resist you if you do not set an active reward methodology.

Reward motivates people, and if there is no motivation, your team will stop to support you over the long term. Your system needs to change in such a way that you will be able to apply changes without resistance. Intrinsic rewards are some of the best motivators for employees. These rewards are rarely monetary. Many times, employees need mental and spiritual rewards to motivate them.

Surprise and fear of the unknown

Your employees may resist you if they do not understand your motivations and your decisions. Fear is not a great leadership tactic and surprising your employees can lead to a lot of negative flak. Your organization needs to be ready for everything, and only a leader can make them ready.

An effective communication channel needs to be established between the leader and the employees else a grapevine of rumors will form creating a serious case of miscommunication. Do not neglect your employees, or they will surely resist you.

Peer pressure

It does not matter if you are an extroverted person or an introverted person; all of us are social creatures. This means that our behavior changes significantly when we are in a group. If a few members in your group resist you, it is possible that all the other members will start resisting you as well due to peer pressure.

The need to belong to a group (within a group) is strong, especially at workplaces. While groups are great for people to feel comfortable, you should still keep an eye on the groups to keep everything under control.

Climate of mistrust

No change or progress can happen when people work in a climate of mistrust. Trust involves honesty, truth, and faith in leaders. Similarly, it involves mutual understanding and faith in the employees as well.

If you want to lead people without resistance, it is necessary to have a connection with them. If your employees trust you, they will not resist you, but if there is an environment of mutual mistrust, your group will never succeed. If you feel that there is a sense of mistrust in your workplace, it is your duty to rebuilt trust.

Trust is both extremely crucial and fragile. It can be harmed easily.

Organizational politics

It is impossible to avoid politics in the workplace. Employees, leaders, top heads, etc. all indulge in workplace politics. Employees may often believe that politics can hinder their progress. They may feel that the leader may misguide them for his or her benefit. This is, again, a classic example of miscommunication and mismanagement. If the communication channel between the leader and the employees is healthy, then there will be no problem between the leaders and the employees.

Fear of failure

Employees and subordinates are often afraid of failure. It is possible that they may resist their leader if they feel that their leader will lead them to fail. They may be worried that if they follow the path shown by their leader, they may enter a world where they cannot succeed.

Fear motivates people, but it can also cause a variety of problems that may lead to failure. If you want to be successful and want your employees to respect you, it is recommended to avoid using fear as a motivator.

Faulty Implementation Approach

Knowledge can be divided into two parts: data and communications. You may have a lot of data, but if you do not know how to communicate it, then your data becomes useless. What you do is important, but how you do it is crucial. Misplaced communication can lead to undue resistance, especially if new changes are brought in in an insensitive manner. Timings are important as well.

Your employees may understand what you want, but they might not appreciate the way in which you want to do the object. You need to think of proper strategies and ideas if you want to implement a change without resistance.

Thus, it is clear that employees do not resist change irrationally. If you can prove to them that you, the leader, is working for their benefit, then they will support you unconditionally.

Final Thoughts on Leadership

Leaders are responsible for their teams and ultimately, the world. Leaders have the opportunity to act in a creative way rather than following an old, patterned, and highly reactive way. Leaders can truly bring in a lot of positive changes in the world if they know their potential and understand the strengths of their group.

A leader needs to be dynamic and active. He or she also needs to be inclusive and understanding because every member of the group possesses some talent and skills. For instance, think that your team is trying to open a huge lock with many keys. Some of the keys are gigantic while some are tiny, but the lock cannot open unless all the keys are inserted in it. Thus, even the tiniest key holds the same amount of respect and importance as the biggest one. A good leader understands this and helps his or her team to grow.

Discarding the myths associated with leadership can help you become bold. It can help you find new horizons and definitions of leadership. It will encourage you and your team to become the very best. Ultimately, leadership is a complex and dynamic concept. There is no one size fits all solution. Every leader has his or her own style, attitude, and approach towards things what is common among all the leaders, though are the myths, which need to be destroyed. Once these are destroyed, you can surely rise to the top along with your team.

Chapter Two: Contexts/Your Position and Making the Most of It

Organizations

Meaning

An entrepreneur is responsible for organizing a variety of factors, including the capital, labor, machinery, etc. He or she does this to channelize these into productive activities. The product travels through a lot of channels and agencies and finally reaches the customers. Business activities can be divided into different functions, and each function is assigned to different individuals as well.

A single person cannot achieve a common business goal; various individuals must come together and make it a success. The organization is this framework where individuals can read come together and divide their responsibilities, duties, and functions. Management is responsible for combining various business activities in the form of predetermined goals.

The contemporary business system is highly complex. To ensure its place in the business world, a business needs to run smoothly. Many jobs need to be performed by many different individuals who are suitable for them. All these authorities need to be grouped into different groups according to functions. The authority and responsibilities are fixed according to their functions.

Concepts of Organization

There are two concepts of organization:

Static Concept

In this, the organization is a structure, a network, or an entity composed of specified relationships. Thus, in the static form, the organization is a group of people who come together and form a formal relationship so that they can achieve a common objective. It is more focused on the positions and not the individuals.

Dynamic Concept

In this concept, the organization is considered to be an ongoing and continuous process. In this concept, an organization is a process in which people, work, and systems are organized. It is related to the process of determining activities that are required to achieve a goal. It also involves the arrangement of these activities into groups so that they can be assigned. This concept considers the organization to be an open and adaptive system. It is not a closed system, unlike the static concept. In a dynamic concept, individuals are the most important aspect.

Management

Management is the art (and science) of getting people together to acquire the same goal using coordination and integration of all the available sources. Management includes all the task and activities that are performed to achieve a goal. These activities include leading, planning, controlling, and organizing.

Management involves decision-making, planning, leading, organizing, and motivating and controlling human resources. It also involves planning and controlling physical and informational resources of an organization to help it to reach the top in an effective and efficient method.

In a broader sense, management is like:

Management is an Economic Factor

I asked an economist; management is one of the major factors responsible for production along with capital, land, and labor. Increase in industrialization is directly responsible for the growth of management. Managerial resources try to decide on profitability and productivity. In such firms, executive development is more necessary as it is directly responsible for rapid progress.

Management is a System of Authority

From the point of view of an administrator, management is like a system of authority. Management was first developed as an authoritarian philosophy in ancient times. Later with time, it developed into a more paternalistic theory. After the paternalistic form, it transformed into constitutional management in which consistent policies and procedures are the major concerns. Nowadays, it has transformed into a more democratic and participatory form.

Modern management is a synthetic combination of all the four approaches mentioned above.

Management is a Class and Status System

Sociologists often refer to management as a class-and-status system. Relationships in modern society are becoming more and more complex, which is why, nowadays, managers are often supposed to be highly educated and brainy. If anyone wants to enter into this class of leaders, you need to be highly educated and earn a lot of knowledge as well. Your education and skills are more important than your political and familial connections. According to some scholars, this is 'Managerial Revolution'.

Management is also a highly individualistic affair, and some people may view it from a different point of view. But the ultimate motive of management is to reach a goal in an efficient and effective manner.

Feature of Management

As said above, management is the process of reaching and setting goals in an efficient and effective manner. This process has certain features or qualities. In this section, let us have a look at these qualities one by one.

Management and Group Efforts

Management is usually associated with group efforts. While people may manage personal affairs individually, in groups, management becomes universal. In every organization, groups are necessary to achieve goals. It has been proven that goals can be achieved with ease if groups are formed.

Management and Purposefulness

Management does not exist without purpose. Management deals closely with the achievement of goals and objectives. The success of management can be measured by comparing the extent to which the goals are achieved. Management is an effective way of achieving goals.

Management and the Efforts of Others

Management is often defined as accomplishing things with the help of others. An organization cannot survive only on the hard work of the manager. Engineers, accountants, salesmen, system analysts, and various other employees all need to put in a lot of work to make an organization successful. All their work needs to be integrated with the work of the manager.

Management and Goal-orientedness

Management is all about achieving a preset goal. Successful managers have a desire for accomplishment. Such managers are aware of where and when to start a process and how to keep it moving as well. Managers are highly goal-oriented, and they know how to influence their group members to become goal-oriented as well.

Management is Indispensable

Management is indispensable, and it cannot be substituted or replaced by anything else. Many people believed that with the advent of computers, managers would become obsolete; however, it was soon proven that computers could only help managers but cannot replace them. Computers can help to widen the vision of the managers and make their insights sharp as well. They allow managers to make decisions quickly. The computer allows managers to conduct analysis that is beyond the normal analytical capacities of a normal human being. In reality, the computer can neither work on itself nor can it pass any judgment. Even the advent of virtual reality and artificial intelligence cannot replace managers. The manager will always be relevant because he or she can use his or her imagination and provide judgment as well.

Management is Intangible

Management is often known as unseen force, and its presence is present in the efforts as well as motivation present in the employees. It is also seen in the productivity and discipline of the group.

Management and Better Life

A manager is responsible for a lot of things. He or she can improve the work atmosphere and can also stimulate group members to perform and work better. He or she can instill a sense of hope in the group members.

Group

Man is a social animal who loves to live in a group. This group can be society, club, family, college, institute, college etc. This instinct is also found in animals such as leopards, elephants, lions, sheep, etc. Leaders are the people who lead the groups. Leaders are supposed to have commitment, vision, and drive to achieve the mission of the group. Team leadership is essentially the management of a group. The leader should be able to inspire and motivate the members of the team. The leader should also be adaptable and flexible.

Group Leadership for Project Management

A project is a particular task undertaken by a group. It can be anything such as software development, construction of a building, managing social parties etc. In the initial phases of the project, a plan is necessary. A plan should include budget, available resources, goal, members, and motive.

Teamwork

The team leader should be able to lead the members of the team effectively. All the individual members of the team should get an environment that is suitable for efficient and effective work. Following is a list of things that are necessary for individual group members.

- Equal opportunities for growth and development for all members of the group.
  o Safe atmosphere to work. This includes physical as well as social and mental safety.
- Respect each member of the group. Respect given is respect gained.
- If conflict ever arises in the group, it should be solved amicably.
  o Regular meetings should be conducted to monitor the progress of the group and should solve the problems as well.
- If a failure occurs, it should be analyzed with proper meetings.
- If success occurs, it should be celebrated.
- A leader should always try to get honest feedback from the group members.
  o Once the feedback is received, it should be analyzed, and corrective measures should be undertaken.

Self-leadership

What is self-leadership?

Self-leadership can be defined as the capability to gain the motivation and direction that can positively influence your performance and work. It is related to mastery and personal excellence. Self-leadership is closely associated with self-confidence, self-efficacy, and your self-beliefs. The confidence and ability to complete goals and tasks is closely related to self-leadership. Self-leadership allows you to become your best self and helps you develop a personal brand as well. It makes you compete with yourself, which can help you to achieve your professional as well as personal goals.

Importance of self-leadership in the current world

Today's world is highly competitive. It changes significantly almost every minute. This means that you need to be unique and remarkable if you want to stand out from the crowd. You need to communicate in an effective, clear, and bold manner so that other people can understand your ideas.

If you want to be a leader, you should create foundations that can help you to display your leadership skills. The team is responsible for the direction, commitment, and alignment. It is true that leadership and self-leadership are different, but they are complementary to each other.

How to achieve self-leadership?

Achieving self-leadership leads to a lot of dedication and passion. Here are some tips that can help you to achieve self-leadership effectively.

Purpose in Life

A self-aware leader should always ask himself or herself a question, 'what is the purpose of my existence?' Without a purpose in life, you are left at the mercy of your fate. Having a clear direction and a sense of purpose keeps you on track and allows you to develop strategies that can help you your goals.

Blind Spots

Blind spots are the aspects of your personality that you are unaware of including feelings and values. You need to become aware of these blind spots. This awareness requires a lot of courage and boldness. It involves getting feedback from others, often from your subordinates. This will help you become more self-aware and ultimately successful as well.

Character Building

Personal character is composed of behavior and mental characteristics. This personal character sets you apart. It displays moral potency and is related to moral efficacy, moral ownership, and moral courage. Character is related to your integrity. Integrity refers to the set of characteristics that define your trustworthiness and credibility. A good leader is supposed to be consistent with their values and promises. Being consistent with your values allows you to be reputable. Reputation is necessary for good leadership; it can even be your most powerful asset.

Ethics and Integrity

If you want to become a self-leader, you need to become selfless. You should be ethical and should possess integrity, as well. You should be fair, honest, and diverse. Ethics are essential and should not be left to chance.

Family

Families are quite similar to organizations, specifically community organizations. There are many different kinds of families, including old fashioned, extended families, modern nuclear families, single parents, childless parents etc. All these variants are commonly seen in the modern world. Almost all these families and their leaders are based around the same principles of leadership. By applying these principles, you can bring a lot of happiness and success for your family.

Importance of leadership in families

There exist many ways in which leadership can help in the maintenance of the family. A family should always support the development and growth of the family members. A good leader can help family members grow in a holistic manner. A good family leader is not only concerned about the materialistic needs of the family members, but they are also concerned with the emotional needs of the family members as well.

Balance

Leadership is essential if you want to balance the different needs of the family members. It is true that the needs of one member may dominate at certain times, for instance, in the case of injury or illness, but with time the normal function of the family must be restored.

Generally, children are the priority of the family as compared to especially. This is especially true in the case of parents.

Another common problem that causes an imbalance in the family is when one adult dominates the whole family. For instance, if the mother (the head of the family) forces her family to live a strange lifestyle of denial and isolation, the family will become miserable. The imbalance is especially bad for children of the family.

Common Goal

Leadership in the family allows setting a common goal for the family. This allows the family to be healthy, happy, and satisfied. Like any other organization, a family needs a vision as well. A family needs to have a mission or a purpose to which its members can subscribe.

This mission is generally the successful growth and development of children.

Creating Leadership in The Family

In regular families, leadership is often owned by the parents. Sometimes this leadership can be held jointly by both the parents and sometimes it can be held by one of the two parents as well. It depends on the parent how he or she approaches leadership. It depends on the leader how he or she handles the responsibilities.

It is necessary to remember that families work like regular organizations as well. The family leader can achieve respect, success, and authority if he or she follows the rules of leadership. The leader of the family should be able to develop the same leadership skills that are required by other leaders. These qualities include open-mindedness, communication skills, fairness, integrity, commitment, and generosity.

CEO

A CEO or the Chief Executive Officer of any organization is a multi-faceted leader who needs to possess a variety of qualities. They are supposed to have many different skills and knowledge.

Initially, organizations would employ those leaders who had pertinent administration experience. Today, they are happy to take chances on leaders who bring distinctive ranges of abilities to the table and utilize those to enable the organization to grow in the modern world.

No one is a born leader. With ample practice and dedication, everyone can learn how to be a great leader. With dedication and practice, a person can gain the skills necessary to be a great leader.

Inspiring people to do things

A leader should be able to light a fire of inspiration in the mind of his or her employees. He or she needs to learn how to communicate in such a way that will inspire people to do their jobs in an efficient manner. CEOs and other bosses need to understand that connecting with employees leads to efficient work and good work ethic. Honesty begets honesty.

Rapidity

As mentioned above, the world is undergoing continuous and rapid change. Change is present in every nook and cranny of the world. The corporate world is undergoing rapid changes in almost all aspects. There are technological changes, financial changes, social changes, economic changes, societal changes, etc. All these changes impact the corporate world and are rapidly causing problems. For instance the problems that were solved over the past few years have now returned with a vengeance. The old solutions have become obsolete. Thus, a leader needs to understand the methodology of change and learn to change with the times as well. He or she should be able to lead his group toward adaptation, change and growth.

Emotional Intelligence

Emotional intelligence as a concept has been discussed in detail in the last chapter of this book.

School Can't make you a great leader. A leader needs to learn their job themselves. Unlike other jobs, leaders are allowed to make very few errors. A successful leader possesses essential skills, such as trustworthiness, vision, acumen, high emotional intelligence, etc. These skills can only be developed with time, practice, and dedication. Good leaders are often great visionaries and can use these skills to help motivate their team.

Chapter Three: Behavioral and Style Theories/ Leadership Development Methods and Tips

In this section, let's take a look at the various styles of developing leadership and how leadership is closely related to other business tactics.

Allegiance and Leadership

Many people feel that loyalty has become a rare commodity in today's world. Backstabbing has become a common phenomenon, and everyone is trying to step on the other person just to reach the top. People have become self-centered and care about nothing but their own benefits. Loyalty and leadership are closely related. A leader cannot succeed if he or she is not loyal to his or her employees and vice versa.

Loyalty and trust can be used in many different ways, but it is also possible to misuse them. Relationships are being degenerated almost every day in today's world, and it is no wonder that loyalty has become an elusive trait. If a leader wants to become a great leader, he or she needs to create an atmosphere where loyalty, trust, and faith hold the center stage. These three factors need to be the rules with no exceptions.

Relationships are, in a way, the currency of leadership. Leaders need to know that loyalty can help their group to grow. Loyalty and leadership go hand in hand. If a leader fails to understand this simple fact, they will not survive in this world. There are many different things that make a leader successful, but loyalty is always the common denominator in all these equations. Loyalty is a two-way street; if the leader is loyal towards the employees, the employees will be loyal to the leader and the leaders agenda. You will receive what you give and vice versa.

It is crucial for leaders to understand the difference between trust-based loyalty and fear-based loyalty. One of them is real and permanent while the other one is fake and temporary.

If people are loyal to you just because you are a leader, then this kind of loyalty will always disappear. If people are loyal to you because you have earned their respect and faith, then their loyalty will never go away.

Being a team manager is a great duty. You can never be a great leader if you believe that being feared is a sign of trust and honor. Employees should respect you, but should never be scared of you. Imposing fear is easy, but earning respect takes a long time. A fear-based style of leadership will never allow trust, loyalty, creativity, innovation, and talent. It will always crush these crucial traits. Fear stifles and hinders people, while loyalty promotes them.

A leader who uses fear-based tactics to control people will always fail. This is because: his or her employees will not give their best performance. When things get tough or when other options are available, the employees will run away and leave the leader alone. If a leader believes that instilling fear in someone's mind is a great way to control them, then you are not a leader; rather you are a tyrannical bully. You will never earn loyalty from your employees.

It is necessary to remember that great people do not consider them to be the masters of the universe; rather they see themselves as inspirational teachers, catalysts, servants, and team builders. There is a huge difference between a leader and a dictator. For instance, the teachers who can inspire students, who can encourage the students to follow their passions, and who can challenge the students in a positive way are the best teachers. If the teacher in a highly dominating way and is too proud, his or her students will despise him or her. He or she will not be appreciated as a great leader.

You may be confused about how to know whether your employees respect you or are they afraid of you.

Tips to Judge

There are five simple tips that can help you to make your judgment.

Yes-men

Leaders who use fear-based tactics to control other people often surround themselves with like-minded people. If they cannot find like-minded people, they tend to surround themselves with a bunch of people who share their views in a vacuum. Everyone likes praise, but false praise instils a false sense of security, which can ultimately lead to a lot of problems. Great leaders will always value the opinion of their group members even if the opinion goes against their decision. Good leaders always keep their ideas open for scrutiny and debate. They encourage their group members to discuss the decisions and ideas.

Interaction

The leaders who use fear-based tactics to control people often avoid interacting with their employees. If you feel that your employees do not interact with you or seek your advice, then it is possible that they do not respect you. They do not treat your decisions as important and believe that your ideas are useless. They may also be afraid of you belittling them. In a fear-based scenario, the employees may think that there is no use of talking to the superiors, so why bother. This lack of interaction is often a result of fear.

Feedback

In the first section, we saw how a good leader puts his or her ideas for scrutiny. Similarly, a good leader also puts himself or herself up for scrutiny. A great leader must subject himself or herself for a 360-review process if he or she ever wants to succeed. Scrutiny allows for developmental opportunities, and it allows people to grow professionally and personally. When you put yourself up for scrutiny, you will not get 100% positive responses. But it is necessary to accept all kinds of responses and evaluate them. This will allow becoming the best version of yourself. If you use fear-based tactics, then you will only receive positive comments, which will be insincere flattery. Flattery is a sign of dishonesty.

Effectiveness

If you cannot retain people, then you are not an effective leader. An effective and great leader has loyal employees who would not leave him or her without any reason. A leader who uses fear-based tactics to lead people will never have a satisfactory team. Their team will consist of people who are not passionate about their work.

Poor Performance

Employees who respect their leaders will always perform better than the employees who are scared of their leaders. Leaders who tend to control and command people with the help of fear rarely do well. If you think that your company is not growing, then it is necessary to check your leadership style. Constant evaluation can help a leader to grow.

Question and Evaluation

Imagine, if your employees hold an election, will you be re-elected once again by a landslide or will they dethrone you immediately? If you choose the latter option, then you need to evaluate your decisions and leadership styles. Things that have been earned like trust, loyalty, and friendship will always outlast the things that have been snatched or forced. People will always stand by you if they truly respect you.

Traits of Leaders Who Inspire Loyalty

Nowadays, modern workers are less likely to retain their jobs and remain at the same company for a long time. People transition from one job to another all the time, but this not because loyalty has become obsolete. Rather the value of loyalty has gone up significantly because now it has become a rare commodity. Many leaders and organizations still try to instill loyalty in their group members. Here are some traits of leaders who inspire loyalty in others.

Authenticity

The leaders who are authentic and honest will always find their subordinates to be loyal and honest as well. No one likes working for fake people. Nowadays the younger generation will look for a new job instead of suffering under a fake person who has little to no respect for them. This means that authenticity has now become a precious factor. People trust authentic leaders because they are accountable for. They act the same way in front of their superiors and subordinates as well. They do not change their 'colours' according to the situation.

Service

The leaders who believe that their job is to guide and motivate the lives of their group members are great leaders, and they will always find loyal followers. For such leaders, team members are more than mere workers; for them, they are real people with real goals. Great leaders understand that they can help these people to achieve their goals.

These leaders try to find the purpose and the meaning behind their employees' goals that can help them to motivate them. Success is a relative term. A group cannot succeed unless everyone participates. A successful group is a group in which every person is trying to grow.

Professional Development of the Employees

Your subordinates will not be loyal to you if you are not willing to mentor them. The best leaders always try to find ways and methods through which their staff members can develop not only professionally but personally as well. The employees who believe that they can develop professionally under a leader will always be loyal to him or her. If the employees act disloyal, then it is due to their leaders not providing them with enough opportunities to grow.

If you want to be a great leader, it is recommended to find opportunities through which you can train and challenge your employees. Normally such resources are available in every company, but if they are not, try to bring them from the outside. Developing and cultivating the talent and skills of your employees will ultimately prove beneficial to the organization.

Display of Trust

Great leaders try to push their group members out of their comfort zone while supporting them thoroughly. If the leader is confident, his or her followers will be confident as well. Such members will be ready to accept any challenge, thanks to the trust and support of their leaders. But this trust cannot be verbal only. You need to display trust through your actions as well. Employees who understand that their leader will support them even if they take on bigger challenges will always be loyal to the leader.

Ideas

Good leaders are always open about their beliefs and ideas. Such leaders often serve as an inspiration to their group members. These leaders display their ideas, thoughts, and decisions openly. If the leader can display what they want in an honest way, their group member will understand the passion of their leader.

Great leaders are unafraid of being wrong or rather being proved wrong. They do not care if they win or lose, but they believe that a healthy debate is necessary for better decisions. They are energetic and understand that if they want the group to succeed, they will have to work together. A despotic leader will never get loyal followers.

They Always Pitch In

Inspiring leaders always try to work with people whom they are supposed to oversee. This creates a sense of camaraderie between the workers and their leader. It also shows how the leader does not consider any work or project to be less important or useless. Nothing is beneath a great leader. If an emergency arises, a great leader will arrive first at the scene and will try to rectify it immediately. They don't expect others to do the tasks that they themselves will not do.

Interest in Employees Lives

People who inspire loyalty are often interested in the lives of others. They can share a lot of information about their group members because they are genuinely interested in their wellbeing. This includes not only their professional life but also their personal interests, family, friends, etc. If you want your employees to be loyal, you need to know them as people. While personal and professional lives are two separate things, both of them influence each other. Supporting and helping an employee in his or her personal crisis will definitely help him or her in their professional life.

People Follow Because They Want To

Leaders are supposed to be the heroes of the corporate world. They encourage us to take risks that we would never take otherwise. They help their groups to produce results. In the corporate world, good leadership can make or break a business. It is no wonder that people spend so much money and time trying to develop leaders.

But often, while trying to understand and grasp the skills necessary for leadership, people tend to forget that there are two facets of the leadership equation. A leader requires more than exceptional talent to attract followers. It has now become significantly difficult to find followers in the modern world. The major problem behind this is that most managerial programs and literature are related only to the qualities of the leader. These texts believe that if you are charismatic, you will attract followers. This is a myth, as a person needs to have a variety of skills to attract followers. Leaders and employees are equally driven by their passions.

There are two motivations behind a person to follow someone; they are rational and irrational. Rational followers are conscious. They understand why they should follow a person. Some major reasons why a person will become a rational follower include status, money, power, or connections. Irrational followers, however, have motives that lie beyond the conventional word. These motivations are often due to powerful images and emotions. These images and emotions are often a result of the subconscious.

It was Sigmund Freud, the father of psychoanalysis who first tried to evaluate followers' unconscious motivation to work. By practicing psychoanalysis for years together, he was confused to see that his patients kept falling in love with him. While most of these patients identified as women, many others identified as men as well. Freud soon realized that this infatuation was not a result of his personal qualities; rather, it was because the patients related him to a past figure in their lives. So, some people related him to their father or uncle, etc. Thus, people were transferring their feeling of love for their parents onto Freud. Freud believed that this phenomenon was universal. He believed that this is the reason why many people choose spouses or partners who are like our parents.

According to Freud, this dynamic is known as 'transference'. Transference is considered to be one of the most important discoveries of Freud. According to Freud, a patient would be 'cured' once they understood their transference. But even today, identifying transference is a difficult objective. It is still considered to be a major goal of psychoanalysis.

Not all transference is positive. For instance, if the employee sees his employer acting like a snob or being rude towards someone, the employee will emulate the employer's behaviour. Transference is not permanent, for instance, an employee may continue to emulate the leader, but if his or her expectations are not met, he or she may end the transference process.

Just because you are a leader does not mean that your employees will follow you or your orders. Anyone can become a leader, but to become a successful leader, you need to work hard to earn the confidence, trust, and respect of people. Only then will you become popular, and people will start taking you seriously.

Anyone can hone their skills to become a great and popular leader. All you need is dedication, passion, and practice. With determination and practice, you will soon become a popular leader.

Tips to Become A Popular Leader

Here are a few things that you should practice to become a popular leader.

Give Respect, Gain Respect

Being respectful is easy when the situation and the person is motivated and mature, but this is rarely the case. Leaders often need to deal with difficult people who will often end up eating your patience and time with strange ideas and requests. Similarly, some employees may get on your nerves as well. In such situations, it becomes difficult to maintain your calm and continue in a respectful demeanor.

True respect does not depend on the situation or the person. True respect is the belief that all human beings are inherently worthy of being respected; this includes people who test your patience as well. This means that you need to treat people in a way that will preserve their as well as your dignity and honour.

When you act respectfully towards every person you interact with, you create an environment of love and caring that soon enveloped your workplace. This atmosphere encourages employees, leaders, and everyone else to treat each other and the clients in a respectful manner. Remember that your employees will always try to imitate you, so if you act respectful, they will act respectfully as well.

Communication

Great leaders understand that communication is the key to leadership. Communicating your ideas in a clear yet concise manner is necessary if you want to avoid any misunderstandings or confusions. While the main focus of communication is to deliver messages, there are many other factors that make communication so crucial for the corporate world.

Communication should always be informative and efficient. It should be used in such a way that it should motivate, inspire, and persuade others. When leaders communicate in a particular way, they can truly enjoy the true results of good communication.

Be Generous

Generosity is often confused with monetary generosity. But this is just one form of generosity. While keeping your employees happy by giving them frequent bonuses, gifts, and promotions is a great way to display generosity, you can display it in various other ways as well.

One of the easiest ways to display generosity is by encouraging and praising your employees liberally. Always praise your employees when they deserve it. Similarly, be gracious if they ever commit a mistake. It also means that you should let go of some control and let others take more responsibilities.

Do not expect something in return while being generous. Try to be self-less, and you will instantly become popular.

Display Your Passion

Passion is contagious. When the leader is excited and passionate about a task, his or her employees will feel enthusiastic as well. But just being passionate will not help you to get others excited; you need to display your passion and enthusiasm.

Expressing your passion will allow your employees to understand how invested you are in a task. They will understand how passionate you are about the task and how important it is for you. By looking at your passion, they will understand that what they are doing is worthwhile and that their work is not useless.

Be Humble

Humbleness is a great way to influence people and become a popular leader. But sometimes humbleness can be confused with being a pushover. Do not let people walk all over you. Be humble but be bold as well. You should take responsibility for your mistakes and should also accept the fact that there are some activities that your employees can do better than you. Nobody is perfect.

Humble leaders are not only more effective, but they are better liked as well. Learning and development take a lot of hard work. Failure is the first step to success. Leaders who can overcome their fears and can move forward are considered to be bold and humble. People love such leaders because they show humane qualities.

Take Responsibility for Your Decisions

Making tough decisions in the times of adversity is one of the most important traits of great leaders. Great leaders will always accept the results of their decisions, whether negative or positive. Even the leader makes a poor decision; he or she needs to accept the result. Accusing others of your own fault will make you an infamous leader.

A great leader should not be afraid of making decisions. He should also be able to take risks. Seeking opportunities and taking responsibilities are two other traits that make great leaders so popular.

Show courage

Displaying courage in times of difficulty is one of the best ways to inspire others. It is impossible to find a person who is not scared of anything. Even the greatest leaders feel afraid from time to time. Leaders are often scared of competition, risks, failure, and similar circumstances. But inspiring leaders will always try to ignore and face their fear and will display courage. Fear produces a lot of energy. This energy can be harnessed and converted into courage. Using this courage, great leaders move ahead and face their fears gallantly. Courage is influential, and group members often feel bold if their leader is courageous.

Courageous leaders understand the importance of their team. They understand that they cannot do anything without their teams.

It is true that becoming a popular leader and getting followers is a difficult task. Not all people can do it naturally, but these skills are not innate, and you can learn them as well. With time and practice, you can learn how to be a popular leader. Just practice the above steps religiously, and you will soon become a great leader.

People Development

One of the most important things that a leader can do for his or her employees is by helping them to develop. Developing employees professionally and personally can help the company to develop as well. When employees are developed, they become more productive, smarter, and bolder. They start performing in a better way. This way, the group will develop. A leader becomes great when he or she changes the lives of other people. Developing people is the best way to change the lives of people.

If you do not know how to mentor and motivate people, here are some tips that can help you get started.

Charity Begins at Home

Before you decide or begin to improve and develop others, you need to develop yourself. If you don't develop others before yourself, you will end up looking like a hypocrite. People will not consider you to be a genuine mentor or leader who is interested in the development of his employees. Employees often follow their leaders, and it is thus necessary to become a good role model if you want your employees to develop. Developing your skills will also help you to become smarter and bolder, and you will be able to develop others in a far more effective way.

Trust and Mutual Respect

Employees should understand that by recommending development strategies, you are not insulting them. Many people avoid visiting developmental seminars because they are afraid that their weaknesses will be exposed. You can avoid this pitfall by building a rapport with them. Try to connect with them and create an atmosphere of trust and faith. Make them understand that you are interested in their development and wellbeing.

Learning Opportunities

Employee development does not happen in the annual review. Similarly, it does not happen in the HR department either. It needs a lot of work, as it is a prolonged process. There are many learning opportunities spread out throughout the office hours. For instance, project check-ins, interactions, talks, and meetings, etc. are all great learning opportunities through which you can develop your employees.

Ask Questions

While dictating is the norm, people rarely perform when they are merely dictated. Dictation rarely creates passionate and involved employees. If you want to involve your employees-ask good questions. By asking frequent and good questions to the employees, you will allow them opportunities through which they will be forced to think on their own and come up with solutions. This will help them learn and develop.

Learn How to Delegate

A lot of leaders often spend the time of work that they should not be doing. It is necessary to learn how to let off responsibilities so that others can take them over. Delegating tasks and responsibilities on your employees will not only make your schedule freer, but it will also provide your employees with opportunities to develop. Thus, this is a win-win situation. The only thing you need to remember is that the results will not be the same. It is possible that your employees may fail at first, but even the failure will help them to develop. Ultimately, they may start to perform even better than you do.

Stretch Assignments

The two best ways to develop and learn in the corporate world are stretch assignments and job change. While job change is not always possible, stretch assignments can help your employees to develop significantly. As a leader, you can find a variety of opportunities for your employees according to their needs. Avoid picking the most qualified person for a job, as this will make them stagnant; instead, pick a person who can learn a lot from such assignments. This will help them develop, and ultimately, you will end up with a team in which everyone will be equally skilled and talented.

Networking Introductions

It is impossible to succeed in the corporate world if you are not well connected. Managers are often well connected. They should use these connections to introduce their subordinates with other people. This will allow them to connect their employees with mentors, experts, and models. Expanding an employee's network can help them to become more skilled and talented. This will also remind the employees that you are not the only person who can help them grow. It will also help you to grow, as you too will cement your relationship with your employee and your contacts.

Feedback

Nobody is perfect, and everyone has a weak spot or two. A bad leader will confront their employees and insult them for their weaknesses. A good leader, however, will try to be tactful and will explain the employee his or her weakness in a calm way. The leader will give well-worded feedback that can help the employee to rectify his or her mistake and avoid it in the future as well.

Organizational Politics and Culture

Politics is often considered to be a dirty field, but it is impossible to escape it in the corporate world. Your staff needs to understand this and look at politics from a positive point of view. They should understand how to navigate office culture. A great way to make your employees politically savvy is using role-playing. Through this method, you can teach the employees the in's and out of the office politics and culture.

Spend Money

Nothing is free in this world, and if you want your employees to grow and develop, you should be ready to invest in them. Some great way to enrich your employees include coaches, training, conferences, workshops, etc. These tangible resources require tangible investment in the form of money. A good training program can work wonders with the employees. It will also help your employees to understand that you appreciate them and are ready to spend real money on their development.

Chapter Four: Leadership Development Methods and Tips

Significant Leadership Behaviors and Attitude

Listening and Communication

Communication is something that sets us apart from all other animals. Thanks to our skills in communication, we can talk, lead and participate in a group. Leaders need to have excellent communication and listening skills if they want to succeed. In this section, let us have a look at some communication skills.

Listening

Listening is perhaps the most important skill a leader can possess. The ability to listen and act upon it is essential for everyone who wants to succeed. Professional listening skills comprise of listening to the message, listening for emotions hidden behind the messages, and understanding the relevant questions regarding the message.

Listening for message includes hearing the facts correctly and understanding them carefully. This includes listening to the messages without any prejudice and prejudgment. You should not be distracted by any thoughts or ideas while listening to the message. Many times, people only concentrate on the words of a message and fail to understand the emotions behind them. This leads to incorrect understanding. You should be able to hear the signs of emotions, especially the changing intonations and rising (or lowering) pitch.

Complimenting

People who believe that employees only work for money do not understand the human psyche. Along with money, people also like to be praised and noticed for their work.

Compliments are especially effective when they are paid in writing, and when they are relevant to the situation. A written compliment stays with the person for a long time, and the person can read it multiple times as well.

This method is great for managers, leaders, supervisors, and everyone else who wants to appreciate their colleagues.

Delegating Tasks Clearly

When you plan a task, you should ideally plan 'what', 'who', 'where', 'when', 'how', and 'why'. These six things should be in your mind when you explain something to another person as well. Explaining the 'why' or the reason behind a task is essential, especially when related to deadlines. It is possible that the employee may not understand that their task is a small part of a grand task. When they understand this, they will work with a new passion and zeal.

Managing Meetings

Understanding how to manage meetings is an essential communication skill that a leader needs to understand. A meeting should be 'good' from the point of view of not only the leader but all other participants as well.

Understanding the value of time of all the participants will allow you to understand the worth of the meeting. If ever you believe that a topic can be discussed and informed using just an email, then conducting a meeting for it is useless.

The purpose of the meeting should always be useful and relevant for everyone. Often you can conduct a proper discussion using just email. Just ask open-ended questions that demand answers. This method works great with employees who are introverts. They may have brilliant ideas, but they may not present them in meetings due to their introversion.

Positive Verbal and Non-Verbal Communication

Communication is not just about words; it is about your emotions, your behavior, your gestures, and your movements as well. Employees pay close attention to their leaders. They analyze and many times, reciprocate and replicate the behaviors of their employers. For instance, if a leader receives bad news and acts violently or too emotionally, the employees will lose respect for the leader. But if the leader acts composed and accepts the news gracefully, he or she will become immensely popular.

Remember to keep a simple smile on your face when you greet someone. This will make you appear courteous.

Communication skills are necessary if you want to succeed in business and want to become a successful leader. The above strategies will help you become a great communicator and in turn, will help you become a great leader as well.

Assertiveness

Many people confuse assertiveness with confidence. Both of these skills are essential if you want to become a successful leader. Assertiveness is a mixture of aggressiveness and passiveness. If you act passive while expressing your views, people will believe that you are submissive. But if you act too aggressive while expressing your ideas, people will think that you are either too hostile or a bully.

Learning to become assertive will help you to express your views without being too aggressive or passive. You will be able to put forward your ideas without offending or confusing anyone.

In this section, let us have a look at some ways that can help you become more assertive.

Understand assertiveness

Before becoming assertive, you need to understand what assertiveness is. Being assertive is considered to be an interpersonal skill that allows you to be confident and bold without hindering the ideas of others or disrespecting them. Assertiveness means that you do not act in a passive or aggressive manner. You act with honesty and directness instead. Assertiveness allows you to be confident and calm while presenting your ideas.

Keep your communication style inline

Assertiveness is closely related to your communication style and methodology. You need to learn how to be respectful towards people and how to communicate this respect as well.

You can show respect through your words, intonations, pitch, gestures, and body movements. Pay close attention to your body language while talking. Your body language and your words should match. People are not mind readers and thus if you want to convey something, do so clearly. Do not expect them to read your mind. When you make a request or present a preference, do so with immense confidence. Always stand or sit straight and smile while keeping a neutral face. Looking people in the eye is a great way of being confident and assertive.

Understand and accept differences

No two people are alike, and everyone is unique and different in their own way. This means that everyone will have a different point of view, and opinions as well. Never be dismissive of anyone's point of view. Just state your own opinion and try to understand the other person's ideas. Never become angry, frustrated, or sad just because somebody else has different ideas. Never interrupt while someone else is talking. Be respectful.

Speak simply and directly

Speaking in a simple and matter of fact tone is necessary while being assertive. You shouldn't imply things or make other people feel awkward. Speaking the truth should not make others uncomfortable. Always be straightforward, direct, simple, and concise. Remember, less is more, especially when you are asserting yourself. Avoid long-winded explanations and keep your requests and ideas to the point.

Exercise the power of "I."

There is no 'I' in a team, but there is an 'I' in assertiveness. If you want to be assertive without being hostile use 'I' statements frequently. Use starters such as 'I believe...', 'I think...', 'I feel...' etc. Do not use aggressive starters such as 'you never...' or 'you always....' These lines can often cause other people problems and leave them frustrated. A frustrated person will not want to have a conversation with you. 'I' statements will allow you to be assertive without alienating others.

Stay calm

Great leaders rarely lose their modicum and calm. Excitement can often come across as aggression. It is necessary to be calm and cool while expressing your ideas. This will make you appear more confident and will help all the other people relax and listen to you carefully. Maintain a positive body language and eye contact while talking to people. Your breathing and intonations should be normal and composed. Be present with each other.

A calm mind leads to a calm speech that in turn leads to calm action. This will keep you and your colleagues composed.

Set boundaries

Boundaries are important, as they are your personal rules. You should have some personal limits that you should avoid crossing. This is true in the case of assertiveness as well. Never allow people to talk over you, but never act like a bully either. Setting such boundaries will help you to understand when to say yes and how to say no.

Assertiveness is a skill that will take time and practice. You should cultivate and hone it slowly. Practice the above techniques every day, and soon you will become more confident, bold, and assertive.

Authenticity

Authenticity makes a leader 'real' and genuine. Authentic Leadership as a theory is still in its infancy; however, people now accept that authenticity can help leaders become more secure, strong, and bold. A practical approach to authenticity can help you become a great leader. There are many different qualities that can help a person become an authentic leader. If a person displays these qualities, their employees will respond in a positive and comprehensive manner. Ultimately it will benefit the organization a lot. The five basic things that can make a leader more authentic are:

- Passion and purpose
- Behavior and values
- Connection and Relationships
- Self-disciplined and consistency
- Compassion and heart

In this section, let us have a look at all of these, one by one in brief.

Authentic leaders display a sense of purpose, and they understand what they want. They also understand the path of their mission. Their purpose becomes their passion. Passionate people love what they do. They are inspired to do their job and care for it as well. Showing passion for the job enables a leader to lead by example. Leaders who demonstrate passion, inspire employees to work with passion as well. This leads to a positive work and job atmosphere. Thanks to the passion, people can brainstorm and find new ideas and ways to succeed.

Authentic leaders demonstrate a sense of value. They understand that their behavior should be based on values and that they should not compromise with their ideals, values, and ideas. Changing one's values according to the situation makes you seem fake. People will find you untrustworthy. The customer is the king, which means that your behavior should be customer-oriented. Similarly, as a leader, you should be considerate about the feelings of others, and this should reflect in your values as well. Taking shortcuts and different routes are fine as long as you do not forgo your ideals for it. Bending the rules for your own gains may give you short-term benefits, but in the long term, it will hinder your progress.

Authentic leaders display a sense of connection and bonding. They create and maintain positive bonds and relationships with their friends and colleagues. They are not only willing to share their ideas and experiences, but they are also humble enough to listen to the experiences of their subordinates. They prefer communicating with others as it allows them to understand people. A good leader needs to be open about things, ideas, and the thought processes behind them. He or she should be able to demonstrate respect towards others' ideas. The more you connect with people, the more they will want to connect with you and will respect you as well. Be open to things, and you will more be committed towards ideas and goals.

Self-discipline is another quality that is essential for leaders. It allows leaders to be focused and determined. It allows them to focus on a goal and move forward on the path towards that goal with total dedication and discipline. They do not falter even if they experience setbacks. They are consistent and are calm, cool, and consistent. They handle a difficult and stressful situation with ease and calm. They try to keep away stress, confusion, and similar problems. Their cool and composed attitude allows them and others to stay on track.

The last quality that makes leaders authentic is their compassion and heart. They are sensitive to the needs and requirements of others. They are always willing to help others. When people are stressed, they try to solve their problems. They help individuals understand the dynamics of groups and teams. They help people to burst their stress. They are genuinely concerned about the wellbeing of their employees and followers.

Overall, all these qualities can make you an authentic leader. Your passion, consistency, behavior, compassion, and ability to connect with people can help you become a great leader. It is clear that an authentic leader not only cares about himself or herself but also cares for his or her job and employees. It allows such people to be productive, happy and focused. It is true that leadership can be a stressful process, but it is still necessary to be composed and calm all the time.

Remember, authenticity can make you a great leader.

Dominance

There are two strategies that leaders and professionals all over the world use to either gain or maintain their status. These two strategies are prestige and dominance. Both of these strategies are tried and tested and prominent throughout the world of business and leadership. Dominance consists of coercion, power, and intimidation in team situations. Similarly, prestige involves skills, valuable knowledge, and respect. It is clear from the above differentiation; prestige is a far more positive way of gaining status. However, the world is not divided into black and white, and thus a leader needs to possess both the strategies. A leader needs to use both the strategies and use them according to situations. Navigating the society is already a difficult task, and as a leader, the difficulty and complexity of this task becomes even more intense.

According to research, both strategies are essential and effective at displaying dominance and influencing other people. Dominance is a great way of gaining power, but it rarely begets respect. It often kills the wellbeing of a team or group. It is true that dominant people rarely enjoy love and popularity as compared to their 'prestigious' counterparts; it has been observed that sometimes a dominant or a dominance-oriented leader is necessary. Sometimes dominance is better suited for a task as compared to prestige.

Dominant workers generally display superiority, arrogance, and conceit. They tend to possess manipulative, aggressive, and disagreeable personality that is not appreciated by anyone. They also tend to have a high score on the 'dark triad' of personality. This dark triad consists of three traits viz. Narcissism, Machiavellianism, and psychopathy.

People who use prestige often tend to display pride and humility. People who have prestige are agreeable. They also have a lot of self-esteem. They tend to display social monitoring skills, a need for affiliation, conscientiousness. They are scared of negative results and evaluation.

In teams, members who are dominant tend to look at others as either foes or friends. They try to analyze whether a person is useful in attaining their own goals or not. They are often hungry for power. People who use prestige instead are more focused on sharing their skills and knowledge with others. It is no wonder that prestige-oriented people are more popular than dominant members in groups.

Leaders who prefer dominance over prestige can go to any length to protect their power. They can even destroy their team and team members to safeguard their interests. They can coerce people with the help of punishment and reward both. For them, talented and strong members of the group are often a threat. They would rather eliminate the threat instead of utilizing them for the interests of the team. They would rather work with an incompetent worker instead of promoting a competent and strong worker. Such leaders often try to prevent associations and bonding among their team. Bonding often leads to the formation of alliances. It is easy to break an individual but breaking an alliance takes a lot of time and efforts.

Prestigious leaders promote positive relationship and bonding among their colleagues and team members. For them, the success of the team matters more than their own personal success. They are more likely to sacrifice their power for the greater good, which makes them immensely popular.

Then why would a group want to work under a dominant leader? Prestige, as it is apparent, is a preferable and comfortable strategy of working in a team. Nobody likes a coercive, power-hungry, aggressive, arrogant, and

Machiavellian leader. But then, research says that people do desire dominant leaders in certain situations.

Groups tend to prefer dominant leaders only when conflicts arise in their group. They also prefer dominant leaders when an outside party attacks the group. The traits of dominant leaders, such as power-hungriness and aggressiveness, are often useful in such situations. In such situations, the skills and traits of a prestige leader, such as altruism are not appreciated. In fact, they can be looked down upon, and such leaders may be considered weak as well. In the face of conflicts, dominant leaders can change and adjust their tendencies slightly according to the needs of their group. Instead of discarding the strongest player of the team (to discard threat) they may promote them to help their team win.

Narcissism

Narcissistic style of leadership involves leaders that are interested in their interests. They tend to prioritize their ideas and gains often at the cost of other people.

Narcissistic leaders are often hostile, dominant, and arrogant. This style of leadership can often turn destructive, especially when the person is driven by a constant need for approval, power, and admiration. While the negative aspects of narcissistic behavior can ruin one's career, the positive attributes can help you develop good leadership qualities as well.

Let us have a look at some common traits that are associated with narcissistic leaders.

Vision

One of the positive aspects of narcissistic leaders is that they lead with vision. They understand the importance of vision and understand how important it is for people as well. Such leaders are able to see the big picture and rarely 'imagine' things. They often attempt to create things that are not already available.

Admiration

Narcissistic people love being admired and adored. They love having star-struck followers and fans. They possess the gift of attracting followers and often they possess many attractive qualities such as developed articulation and verbal skills. These leaders are often great orators and can deliver extremely moving speeches. They are charismatic and bold.

Criticism

A negative trait associated with these leaders is that they are extremely sensitive. They are especially sensitive to harsh criticism and can barely tolerate it. Unlike other leaders who receive criticism in a constructive way, narcissistic leaders often brood over it. They do not like dissenting opinions and despise slights. They act abrasively towards people who go against them or have a negative opinion about them or their work.

Lack of listening skills

Narcissistic leaders are self-centered, and they rarely pay any attention to others and their ideas. They do not possess good listening skills and open talk about them and their ideas only. This disinterest in listening often results in the formation of a defense mechanism that they use against criticism.

Narcissistic leaders often do not care about their subordinates and their contributions. They do not pay attention to the opinions of others.

Relationships

Healthy narcissistic leaders often show real concern about others. They also respect others' values, ideas, and opinions. Destructive narcissistic leaders, however, do not care for the opinions of others. They will often demean them and their ideas without any sense of guilt or remorse.

Consistency

A leader who possesses healthy levels of narcissism also possesses a set of values that they strictly adhere to. They follow a pre-planned path and rarely go haywire. Destructive narcissistic leaders, in turn, change all the time. They have no values and are known to be fickle. They are also easily bored, as well.

Large projects

Narcissistic leaders dream of building empires (and even taking over the world). They believe that leaving a legacy after them is a must. They often seek endeavors that can help them do this. They often hire subordinates and make plans that will help them reach their dreams. A narcissistic leader will not stop and will continuously create new endeavors and companies.

Empathy

Narcissistic leaders crave understanding and empathy from others; however, they rarely get it. Similarly, they are rarely empathetic towards others as well. Many popular and successful narcissistic leaders are known for their non-empathetic nature. Lack of empathy can prove to be a pro as well as a con. While lack of empathy can help you be practical and strong in the time of chaos, it can also trample upon the feelings of subordinates and employees.

Competitive

As it is clear from above, narcissistic leaders are extremely competitive. They are ruthless and will pursue victory in a bold and relentless manner. They take everything seriously. Even the simplest games can become a matter of life and death for them. A lot of narcissistic leaders do not show remorse and do not care about conscience either. Due to this, they often try to grab victory using licentious ways as well.

Lack of mentoring skills

Many narcissistic leaders lack empathy and are often self-centered; this is why it is almost impossible to find a narcissistic leader who is also a good mentor. Similarly, such leaders cannot be mentored as well. When they do mentor someone, they do not coach people, they just instruct. They cannot tolerate their protégés to become bigger than them.

Don't Use Fear

Fear is a popular workplace tactic, but not many people acknowledge it as it is often hidden. On the surface level, fear is rarely visible, but it often has deep roots in the core of the organization. Fear is not easy to pinpoint but still has a significant influence on the organization. Fear is often generated and spread from people in leadership positions.

The opposite of leading by fear is leading by respect. Both these methods may seem to be similar on a superficial level; however, they are two different methods that lead to vastly different results.

Leading with fear can lead to some short-term benefits. It can lead to immediate action and can also create a sense of urgency and anxiety, which can lead to activity. But such activity rarely leads to a lot of productivity. Leaders do not often use fear to control people; only leaders who are desperate use it as a last resort. This dark side of leading can often lead to a lot of problems. This is why respect-based leadership is often promoted as a healthy alternative to fear-based leadership. Respect-based leadership has enormous benefits and can lead to a lot of positive results. You can begin using this kind of leadership right away, and you will soon start noticing the positive effects.

Let us have a brief look at the key traits of both these leadership styles. This section will allow you to understand the difference between these two and will prove how 'respect' can help you more than 'fear'.

Fear Disempowers

Fear-based leadership creates employees who are self-centered. They only care about themselves and rarely focus on others. People who are motivated by fear rarely look beyond them. They instinctively go into survival mode. They only care about their own jobs. They do not care for the outcome of their organizations and their customers as well. This creates a bad working atmosphere where every employee ultimately becomes narcissistic and self-obsessed. The company's focus changes from profit and customers.

Respect Empowers

Good leaders create good employees. They find methods that allow them to discover best in people. They allow employees to use their full potential. Their energy is desirable. They are inspiring and allow others to go beyond their limits. They do not use coercion to make others work. Inspired leaders create inspired employees and inspired employees to inspire other employees as well. This, in turn, creates an atmosphere of positivity in the company.

Empowered employees' focus externally. They tend to look for out of the box solutions. They like to create a better working atmosphere and like to create better teams as well.

Fear: Lack of creativity and communication

People who lead with fear often create cynical, anxious, and intimidated employees. Such employees rarely trust their leaders and are often toxic to their teams. Fear breeds dishonesty and lack of transparency in the team. Both these factors are essential if you want communication to be successful among your team. If employees are too afraid to bring something up, an aura of dysfunction will settle on the organization. Fear limits rationality. Limited rationality leads to poor decision-making and can truncate action as well.

Fear often leads to concerned and troubled employees. Such employees do not enjoy their jobs, and they are often looking for other options. This behavior rarely leads to successful and innovative ideas. It also creates a stagnant and useless staff. People lose their ability to be creative and innovative. Both these factors are essential if you want to succeed, especially in the modern world. Companies with 'scared' employees can rarely succeed in the competitive world of entrepreneurship. Feat kills imagination and ingenuity. Fear takes away the right of thinking in a free and independent way. If your company uses this method for a long time, your opponents will rise above you.

Respect: Creativity and Communication

Respect is a great way to lead people. Respect always begets respect. Powerful and bold leaders always put their team and team members first. This allows them to win their trust and confidence. The employees who trust their leaders can initiate open communications with them.

Another aspect of respect is becoming a team player. Instead of being 'leader' all the time, you should allow others to voice their opinions, ideas, and feedback as well. You should also ask your team members to pinpoint your weaknesses and allow them to solve them. Be authentic while doing so, or your employees will lose their trust in you. Your team should believe and understand that you are not just and authority figure and that you are a real, approachable human being with whom they can communicate.

Fear Is a Disguise

Leaders often use fear-based leadership because they want to hide their insecurities and fear. Many leaders are aware of this, while many others do it subconsciously. A leader generally uses this method to hide behind a secure wall of intimidation. He or she can appear tough, but on the inside, he or she is broken and scared. This kind of approach soon makes the employees doubt their own skills and creates an overall lack of confidence in the group.

Respect Is Genuine

Leaders who are genuinely respected do not stop until they have achieved their goals. They continue to persevere and are passionate about their work. They hold their employees in high esteem. Great leaders can not only inspire others, but they can also motivate them to do jobs that the employees did not think they could do. They gain respect by leading by example.

Respected leaders are passionate about their group and the purpose behind their group. Their passion is often contagious, and the group members try to emulate this. The members do not care for the title of their leader, even if the title is revoked, the person will still be respected. Even the leaders don't care about the position are driven by their passion for their work.

Fear-based leadership really is not leadership as it is mainly focused on bossing and dominating others. A leader who uses this technique just barks around orders and looks at his employees as commodities that can be expended. They only seek validation and recognition. They use threats to manage people.

Real leaders can inspire and empower people around them with the help of purpose and passion. They guide people by leading by example.

Eliminating Negativity

Negativity is a virus that can lead to a severe infection that ultimately can even destroy and organization. Everyone is highly susceptible to negativity, but people who are uncertain are especially susceptible to it. Uncertainty can make us panic and make rash decisions.

Our brain works continuously on Bayesian inferences. This means it keeps a close eye on the surrounding world and its workings. Your brain observes the world and creates an imaginary model in your head. It uses this model to make predictions about reality. When these predictions clash with the 'real reality', the brain tweaks the model and gets everything running once again. While our brain can handle simple clashes, it cannot tolerate frequent and constant clashes. If it cannot predict what will happen next, you start to panic. Uncertainty thus is the main cause behind panic.

While all kinds of uncertainty lead to panic, 'irreducible uncertainty' is the main culprit. This uncertainty represents the uncertainty in while you cannot do anything about a situation. Uncertainty creates a sort of chain of toxic negativity.

There are many different ways of reducing or minimizing negativity. Let us have a look at a five-step solution for this problem in this section.

Define the way

Before you even begin, it is necessary to remind yourself of what you are supposed to do and how you should do it. You should also keep in mind how and why are you supposed to do the thing. This will enable you to control your employees without making them feel miserable.

Defining the territory

Once you have defined a path, it is now time to define territories as well as the roles of people. All your team members or employees need to know their duties and what is expected of them. This will allow you to keep your employees in control.

Defining your thoughts

A leader should always be open about his or her thoughts, ideas and decisions. He or she should not hide them, or the employees will not find their leader trustworthy. Your employees need to be reassured about your views and ideas frequently. They also need to be reassured about their future in the company.

Defining your cooperation

Be genuine. Nobody likes fake people. It is recommended to listen to your employees, as this will enhance their trust in you.

Define the culture

Instead of focusing on negativity, try to formulate a culture of optimism and positivity. Our surroundings play a major role in deciding our behavior. The more optimistic the atmosphere will be, the more positive you will act.

Chapter Five: Leadership Styles

Leadership is a highly unique and individualistic concept. Its facets and traits change according to individuals, yet it is possible to divide it into certain groups using common characteristics. In this section, let us have a look at some of the most common forms or styles of leadership.

Autocratic or Authoritarian Style

Autocratic style of leadership is also known as the authoritarian leadership style. It is known for its individual control on decisions in which little to no input is desired from the group members. Autocratic leaders generally make choices based on their judgments and ideas. They almost never accept advice from their followers. Autocratic leaders prefer authoritarian and absolute control over their team.

Autocratic leadership style may seem to be a bit erratic, but it has a lot of benefits as well. Often people who use this approach a lot are considered to be dictatorial or bossy, but such behavior can also have a lot of benefits in certain situations. It depends on the user when to use the authoritarian style of leadership. Using it in the wrong situation can lead to a lot of problems as well. Using this type of leadership in an unknown group or situation can be especially harmful.

Characteristics of Autocratic Leadership

Here is a list of some of the primary characteristics of autocratic leadership

- Leaders make all the decisions.
- Almost no input is desired or accepted by the team members.

- Team members are not trusted with important tasks and decisions.
- All processes and methods are dictated by the leader.
- Work is rarely creative.
- Work is often rigid and structured.
- Rules are crucial and are followed with dedication.

Benefits

Here is a list of benefits of the autocratic leadership style.

- This type of leadership provides a lot of oversight and a clear chain of command.
- Leaders make quick decisions, especially in difficult situations.
- Is excellent in situations where strong leadership is required.

As said above the autocratic style of leadership may sound to be negative and useless. It is true that it may lead to negative implications when it is applied to wrong situations or is overused, but it can also lead to a lot of benefits. For instance, when a leader needs to make a quick decision, it is always better to use the autocratic method instead of holding long discussions with the team members. Certain difficult projects may require a strong and autocratic leader for efficiency and success.

If the leader is the most knowledgeable and experienced person in the group, then, it is best to use the autocratic style.

Uses

The autocratic style of leadership can be quite effective in small groups where leadership is absent or negligible. For instance, it can be really beneficial for student groups/

coworkers who are not at all organized. This will not only lead to personal problems but can also cause havoc in the group dynamics. In such situations are strong, and autocratic leader can take charge of the group and change it for good. He or she can help and segregate the tasks. He or she can also help with the deadlines.

Certain group projects work best when a person is assigned to be the leader or if a person himself or herself takes up the role of the leader. This method can help you to assign tasks, set clear goals and roles etc. This way, the group will be able to finish the project on time, and all the members will be able to contribute equally as well.

This style of leadership is also suitable in situations where a lot of pressure is involved. Certain situations like military conflicts are quite stressful and require immediate attention. In such situations, it is necessary to use the autocratic style of leadership. This way, each member of the group will be able to pay close attention to specific tasks and will be able to make complex decisions quickly.

This kind of leadership can also help team members to become highly skilled at performing certain duties. This is great for the health and development of the group.

Another field that can really benefit from the autocratic style of leadership is construction and manufacturing. In this situation, each person needs to have a clearly assigned task, rules, and deadline that they need to follow. An autocratic style of leadership can work wonders in such a situation because it will keep away the accidents and injuries.

Drawbacks

Here is a small list of all the problems associated with autocratic leadership

- The group is not allowed to present its views.
- Is bad for the morale of the team members.
- Can lead to resentment.
- May lead to the death of creativity.

As it is clear from the last section that the autocratic style of leadership can be quite beneficial at times, however, it is still quite problematic and can lead to a lot of problems in many situations.

People who misuse this style are often seen to be controlling, bossy, and dictatorial. This creates resentment and problems among the group members. Group members can feel that they have no say or input in any of the things. This feeling is especially strong in members who are capable and skilled. If they are not allowed to use their pros in a constructive way, their potential remains unused.

Problems

Some of the most common problems associated with autocratic leadership include:

1. It does not encourage group input, as autocratic leaders tend to make decisions without consulting with others. The team members may not appreciate this as they may feel that they cannot contribute their ideas. Autocratic leaders often destroy creativity. This may affect the performance of the team in a negative way.

2. Autocratic leaders often overlook the expertise and knowledge of their group members. They avoid consulting their group members while making decisions that can lead to the failure of the group.

3. Autocracy can also cause problems with the morale of the group. People tend to perform better when they are happy and pleased with their atmosphere. Happiness is often derived when people

believe that they are helping their group and are doing something worthwhile. Autocracy takes away this feeling that makes employees stifled and dissatisfied.

Autocratic Leaders: Survival Guide

As it is clear that the autocratic style of leadership can really work wonders in some situations, but in others, it can cause a lot of problems. It is not an appropriate approach for all situations and groups. If you are an autocratic leader or this happens to be your dominant style, there are certain things that you need to consider to make your style more friendly and open.

Listen

Listen to your group members. This does not mean that you should always follow or use their advice, but listening can still help. Your subordinates will start feeling that they are valuable and hold some importance in the group. If you do not listen to your team members, they will often feel rejected or ignored. Keeping an open mind will make your group more pleasant and productive.

Rules

If you want your team members to follow your rules, you need to establish them firmly in the beginning. You need to ensure all the guidelines are in check and well established. Check whether your team members know that they need to follow the rules.

Knowledge and Tools

Provide your group members with the tools and knowledge that they need. Offer them assistance whenever required. Also, offer them opportunities to get training and take courses.

Reliability

Reliability is the key in any relationship, including leader and employee. If you are not reliable, your team members will quickly lose respect for you. If you expect your group members to follow the rules, you should follow them as well.

Success

Always praise your group members whenever they deserve it. Constant criticism will break their morale.

Autocratic leadership is a strict no-no for many, but you can cherry-pick certain elements from this style to make your own leadership style more potent. You just need to understand the style and use the elements wisely. If you maintain a balance between the democratic and autocratic style, you will be able to lead your group in a better way.

Participative or Democratic Style

Participative style of leadership is also known as the democratic or shared style of leadership. In this style, the group members take an active part in the decision-making processes. This style is versatile and can be used in many different scenarios, including government, businesses, schools etc.

In this style, every member of the group is allowed to participate in the group and exchange their ideas freely. In this method, ideas are allowed to flow freely, and everyone is treated equally. The leader is supposed to offer guidance to the group. He or she is the person who decides the sequence of ideas and what decisions should be made.

According to various studies, democratic leadership is one of the best and effective types of leaderships. It is productive and can allow all the members of the group to participate in important decisions. It can also help the morale of the group.

Characteristics

Here are some of the primary characteristics associated with this kind of leadership:

- Encouragement: In this style, members are encouraged to share their opinions and ideas. (The leader has the final say.)
- Engaging: This style of leadership is far more encouraging and engaging.
- Creativity: In this style, creativity is not only encouraged, but it is also rewarded.

Traits

Following are the traits that are commonly observed in democratic leaders:

- Honesty: Democratic leaders are reliable and honest.
- Intelligence: It takes a lot of intelligence to listen and understand the views of others and then make a wise decision using the views. Democratic leaders are smart and intelligent.
- Courage: Listening to others and using their ideas can lead to a lot of potential problems. Democratic leaders thus need to be courageous.
- Creative: A democratic leader and a democratic group are supposed to be creative.
- Competent: A leader should be competent if he wants to use the democratic style of leadership.
- Fairness: A democratic leader needs to be fair so that he or she can listen to the views and ideas of the group member with patience.

Strong democratic leaders can instill respect and trust in their followers. They are sincere because they often base their decisions on values and morals. They are inspired and love to contribute to the group. Good democratic leaders use diverse opinions and rarely silence dissent. Many democratic leaders prefer dissent over sycophancy.

Benefits

Here is a list of all the benefits associated with a democratic style of leadership:

- Creative solutions and more ideas.
- Group members are committed.
- The group is more productive than other methods.

As group members are encouraged to share their ideas and thoughts in this style of leadership, it often leads to more creative solutions and better ideas. Group members appreciate working in a democratic group because they feel more involved. This way, they care about the end results are thus committed to the projects as well.

Drawbacks

Here is a list of all the drawbacks of the democratic style of leadership:

- Failure related to communication.
- Problems in decision making because of unskilled group members.
- Minority opinions are ignored.

It is true that the democratic style of leadership is considered to be one of the most effective styles of leadership, but it still has some drawbacks. For instance, in situations where the roles are unclear, the democratic style of leadership will almost always fail. In some cases where the group members lack the necessary skills or knowledge, they will not be able to make quality contributions to the group.

Where to Use Democratic Leadership

Democratic leadership can be used in a lot of situations nowadays. It works great in a talented and highly skilled group. It allows people to contribute and is thus great in schools as well.

Laissez-faire or Free-rein

Laissez-faire leadership is also known as a delegative style of leadership. It is a hands-off style of leadership in which the group members are allowed to make the decisions. According to researchers, this style of leadership is the least productive of all other styles of leadership.

While it is known to be less productive, it still has some positive aspects. There exist certain settings where this kind of leadership can work wonders.

Traits of Laissez-faire Leadership

This type of leadership is well known for the following things:

- Guidance: In this style of leadership employees do not receive guidance from their employers.
- Freedom: This method provides total freedom to the group members.
- Provisions: The leaders of these groups only provide the necessary resources and tools to the members.
- Solutions: The group members are expected to use the above resources. The employees are supposed to use their experience the provided resources to tackle the problems.

- Power: Members of these groups are handed over power by the leaders, but the leaders are still expected to take responsibility for the group and the decisions made.

There have been many famous politicians, entrepreneurs, and great leaders who have used certain elements from this method. For instance, Steve Jobs used to give his team members some directions while the members were supposed to come up with ideas and solutions themselves. Similarly, former President Herbert Hoover was well known for his 'relaxed' approach towards governing.

Benefits

Like all the other styles of leadership, this method too has many benefits as well as drawbacks.

1.   The Laissez-faire style is particularly effective if it is used correctly in the right situations and with the right groups.

2.   This method is especially suitable for people who possess skills and creativity. If the group members are motivated, skilled, and capable of independent work, then a Laissez-faire leader will help them achieve success. Such groups require little to no advice and guidance and are thus self-sufficient.

3.   This method is also suitable for groups where the members are more skilled than the leader. As the team members are experts of the area, the Laissez-faire style can allow them to illustrate their knowledge about the topic and skills related to the subject.

4.   In situations where independence is valuable, this method of leadership can work really well. The autonomy of this leadership style allows people to be more satisfied with their job. This style of leadership is

especially great for groups where the group members are motivated and passionate about their jobs.

5.   The leaders who follow this style are often available for feedback and consultation. These leaders can provide insight and guidance at the beginning of the project and then allow the group members to do their job on their own.

6.   This kind of leadership needs a lot of trusts. Leaders should feel confident about the skills and achievements of their group members. They need to be aware of their knowledge, as well.

Negative Aspects of the Laissez-faire style:

This style of leadership is not recommended for situations where the group members do not possess the necessary skills, experience, and knowledge to make decisions. This style is notorious for producing bad performance, bad results, and low group satisfaction.

Not everyone is great at setting their own deadlines and managing their own projects. People often find solving their own problems difficult as well. In such situations, the project may soon go off-track, and the group may miss crucial deadlines.

No role awareness

The Laissez-faire style of leadership can lead to a lot of problems in some situations because, in this style, the roles are not defined within the group. Team members receive little to no guidance and are often unaware of the things that they are supposed to do.

Lack of involvement

The leaders who follow this style of leadership are often withdrawn and uninvolved. This can lead to confusion. The group members may think that the leader does not care about what is happening in the group. This makes the members unconcerned as well.

Low accountability

It is easy to abuse this method of leadership. Leaders may use it to avoid personal responsibilities. If the goals are not achieved, the leader can simply blame the team members and accuse them of not finishing their tasks.

Passivity and avoidance

This style of leadership can lead to lethargy and passivity. People can even avoid leadership altogether. Such leaders will avoid doing anything to motivate their group members and will make no attempt to involve them in-group decisions.

If the group members are unskilled and are unfamiliar with the task of the process, it is recommended to use a more hands-on approach. With time the group members will gain more expertise, and the leader can then switch back to a more laid-back style of leadership that will allow the group members more freedom and independence.

Where to Use Laissez-faire Approach

If you are a Laissez-faire leader, then there are some situations and areas where you can do wonders. This method is well suited for a creative field where people are highly motivated, creative, and skilled. This method can lead to great results in such fields.

For instance, a delegative leader will work great in product design and related fields. In such fields, all the team members are highly creative and well trained. They require little to no management (or assistance). An effective Laissez-faire leader will just provide minimal guidance and oversight to the team members, and the team will still produce great results.

Laissez-faire leaders are generally great at providing the initial data and background to begin a project. This information is great for teams that are self-managed. By providing the team members all the information and tools that they need at the beginning of the assignment, the team will understand what they are supposed to do and will figure out how to do it.

While the Laissez-faire method is great in such groups, it is still recommended to use different leadership methods in different phases of the assignment. For instance, this method can be used in the initial stage of the task, i.e. in the brainstorming session. Later it is recommended to use a more insightful and 'directive' style of leadership.

This style may prove to be difficult in situations where a lot of precision, oversight, and attention is required. In situations where every detail needs to be perfect and timely, this method will fail. In such situations, it is better to use a more managerial or authoritarian style instead. Utilizing the Laissez-faire method in this scenario can lead to a lot of problems, including poor performance, missed deadlines, and lack of direction. This is especially true if the group is unskilled.

It is true that the Laissez-faire method is usually considered to be a style of leadership that can have can negative implications. Yet it can prove to be highly beneficial in many different situations. It is especially useful in groups where all the members are equally skilled and motivated. In such groups, this method can lead to the best results possible. Team members are allowed to use their freedom and are not micromanaged like all the time, so they feel more creative and inspired.

If you are this kind of leader, try to think of situations where you can use this method freely. In groups where more insight is needed, it is recommended to pair this method with some other form of leadership, such as the democratic or the authoritarian method. By examining your own style of leadership, you can become a great leader.

Task-oriented and relationship-oriented

As explained above, leadership varies a lot from person to person. It is subject to the individual's attitude, their surroundings, the atmosphere, etc. It also depends on how they implement plans, how they provide direction, and how they motivate people. In every business endeavor, the style of leadership changes and fluctuates significantly.

Around 83% of organizations believe that it is necessary to develop leaders at all levels. Around 43% of organizations have made it their top priority to bridge the gap between all leader levels. More and more money is being spent on the development of leadership as compared to any other area. Still, around 71% of organizations do not believe that their leaders can lead their organization into the future. If you want to make the best decisions in your training, then it is necessary to know which style of leadership you currently possess and how you can adjust it to enhance the overall performance of your organization.

The two most commonly used and seen styles of leadership are task-oriented leadership and people-oriented leadership. People-oriented leadership is also known as a relationship-oriented leadership style. These two have been a hotly debated topic since forever. Each style has its own pros and cons. In this section, let us have a look at the pros and cons of both the methods.

Task-Oriented Leadership Advantages and Disadvantages

Pros

There are several characteristics and traits that make task-oriented leaders the best leaders around. These leaders are highly proficient and can get things done on time. These leaders create easy to understand and follow methods and instructions due to which their group finishes work on time. This style of leadership is great if you want to maintain high standards of optimal efficiency. Employees who desire structure and do not well on their own can really benefit from this kind of leadership, as it is task-oriented, organized, and structured. It is also deadline-driven, which makes it efficient.

Cons

Some of the most common cons of this style of leadership include lack of autonomy and independence for employees. Employees are not allowed to show their creativity in this method. This can lead to dropping in the morale of the group. When an employee is forced to work in a strict atmosphere with strict deadlines, the company culture goes down significantly. Many employees can become rebellious in such situations, especially if they are skilled and self-motivated.

Another negative aspect of this kind of leadership style is that it hinders creative thinking. It can cause a negative effect on the company's products and its image. It kills innovation and is thus not recommended for companies that are closely related to arts.

Focus

1. Finishing Jobs: This style of leadership is thoroughly focused on finishing the project at hand as soon as possible.

2.   Effective goal setting: For this method to work, the leader sets the goal and formulates a path to reach the goal in the initial stages. This keeps the team focused.

3.   Schedules: This method is highly focused on deadlines and keeping schedules.

4.   Goals: As said earlier, this method is extremely goal-oriented and strives hard to produce the desired results.

People-Oriented Leadership Advantages and Disadvantages

Pros

People-oriented style of leadership is the best for employees as they enjoy the central place in this style. This style tries to appreciate the workers for the work they do. It focuses heavily on employee and employer relationship. This makes the employees think that they are a crucial part of the company, which in turn makes them passionate and motivated. They believe that they can help the company and the group become a great success if they put in efforts.

Cons

This style of leadership comes with many different challenges. It is possible that the employees may end up feeling burdened with responsibilities. They may feel overwhelmed and confused. Some employees cannot work without directions, and such employees will struggle a lot under a people-oriented leader. Many ineffective decisions can be made due to inconsistent skills of the team members. The business may suffer a lot of certain aspects of finance are neglected.

Focus

1. Workers: In this style of leadership, the satisfaction and wellbeing of the workers are considered to be the most important aspect. This method is concerned with the workers and their mental and physical health and whether they are feeling motivated or not.

2. Interaction: This method focuses on conversation and connection between colleagues. It facilitates positive interaction between colleagues, which can produce productive results.

3. Team building: To facilitate interaction between colleagues, this method focuses on team-building exercises and conducts various meetings frequently.

Thus, it is clear that you cannot be task-oriented as well as people-oriented at the same time. You need to decide which path to choose else you will end up being a confused and failed leader. The best way to be a great leader is by picking up the best parts from each style of management and leadership. This will help you to make a combination of various skills and styles that will allow you to cultivate a great persona and working atmosphere as well. Different situations need different approaches. If you keep the pros and cons of all the styles in mind, you can always find the best-suited approach for a situation. Ultimately you will be able to develop a style of leadership that will be unique, personal, and well cultivated and calculated.

Paternalism

Paternalism or paternalistic leadership is a type of leadership style that consists of a dominant authoritative personality who often acts as a patriarch or a matriarch and treats his or her employees as members of a large family. In turn, the employees trust and obey the leader and are loyal towards him or her.

This type of leadership style creates and amicable atmosphere at the workplace in which the employees consider the leader and other employees as their family. Everyone wants to be a part of a family; it is just our natural human tendency. Like families, we have heads in organizations who hold an authoritative position. These leaders decide what is best for the team and make decisions accordingly. This is why in this method it is necessary for the leader to be caring and optimistic.

Elements of Paternalistic Leadership

This kind of leadership is highly common in Asian nations. In fact, it is believed that this style originated in China. This style of leadership consists of three main elements, they are:

- Autocratic leadership
- Benevolent leadership
- Moral leadership

Let us have a look at them one by one.

Autocratic Leadership

The historical as well as the philosophical background of this kind of leadership can be traced back to Confucianism in China. In this style, every leader possesses the legal right to make decisions and the employees must follow it. The employees are bound to obey their superiors. Leaders of this style tend to monitor their workers closely. They always have the last say in things.

Benevolent Leadership

This too finds references in the ancient Chinese texts. In this style the leader is focused on the familial as well as personal wellbeing of the followers. This is done in a holistic and individualistic style. This the most preferred style of leadership as compared to the other two.

Moral Leadership

In this style, the moral character of the leader and his or her potential is used as a role model by his or her followers. Moral leaders show a lot of respect, kindness, and optimism. They treat people in a non-abusive and fair manner. The main goal of this style of leadership is to serve. Rather than showcasing what they can do, the leaders try to develop the capabilities of their colleagues.

Core Characteristics of Paternalistic Leadership

Paternalistic style of leadership has many traits. Let us have a look at them one by one.

Compassion

A leader cannot be paternalistic if he or she is not compassionate. This element is essential as it enhances the loyalty of the employees towards the organization. Employees are important in a paternalistic style of leadership, and it is the duty of the leader to make the employees feel comfortable and valuable. A leader cannot make his or her followers feel, so unless he or she possess empathy and compassion.

Compassion is innate, but it can also be learned. Compassion meditation is a great way to learn compassion in an altruistic and easy way. If you include compassion mediation in your daily schedule, you will start feeling compassionate for people soon. It will allow you to connect to the feelings of the people, and it will also show how trustworthy you are.

Good Organizational Skills

A paternalistic leader needs to have good organizational skills. They should be able to set their priorities straight while making decisions. Without good organizational skills, their group will not be able to achieve success.

Decisiveness

In this style of leadership, the power to make decisions is completely vested with the leader. Due to this, the leader needs to have a lot of potential, knowledge, and expertise, to make correct decisions. If you follow this style, you cannot contemplate (or make regretful) decisions, as it will hinder the progress of the group.

Making decisions and moving forward is not an easy task, as it requires a lot of thinking and judgment. Remember, with great power comes even greater responsibility.

Empowerment

This style of leadership is highly focused on bringing the best out of the employees. As a leader who follows this style of leadership, you want your employees to grow and develop, just like a parent. Similarly, you want to see your employees succeed and achieve their goals. You also want them to grow as an individual and grow professionally as well.

Empowerment needs a careful balance between micromanagement and autonomy. This kind of leadership does not give the employees a lot of authority, and the leader is supposed to make decisions. The leader, however, does not question the actions of the group members.

Influence

In this style of leadership, it is necessary for the leaders to influence the subordinates. This style provides the leader with a lot of power. While it is strictly not an authoritative style of leadership, the leader still possesses the power to make decisions and change them as well.

There are many different ways in which you can influence people. You can influence people with your knowledge and communication skills. You can also influence them with your wit and charm.

Limitations of Paternalistic Leadership

Let us have a look at some of the limitations of this type of leadership:

1.   Morale: This style can lead to dropping in the morale of the employees, as they are not allowed in the decision-making process.

2.   Dependency: The group members in this style are dependent on the leader as it is the leader who makes all the decisions.

3.   Inclination: It is possible that the subordinates may feel less inclined to find solutions because they will feel less involved.

4.   Irrational Outcome: It is possible that some group members will not be satisfied with the decision of their leader but will still have to follow it.

5.   Struggle: In this style, barring the leader, no other roles are defined properly. Due to this, a lot of internal struggles and issues may arise and disturb the modicum of the group.

Examples

Let us have a look at the paternalistic style of leadership being used in real life:

Executive Leadership

In this style, the employees are considered to be important, and their needs are valued over others. The firm can go to great lengths to avoid layoffs even if the business is losing money. It believes that employees are critical to the health of the firm.

Governments

A government that follows this style of leadership will often try to make quality goods free of cost. It will also try to bring down the costs of products by providing subsidies. These governments often levy heavy duties and taxes on 'harmful' substances, including tobacco, alcohol, etc. This kind of government is associated with regulations, rules, and it tries to control every aspect of the lives of its subjects.

Management

A manager who follows the paternalistic style of leadership will try to boost and develop his or her employees by providing them with opportunities where they can grow. He or she will try to provide them with opportunities that suit their talents and interests. This way, the manager can create a loyal and powerful workforce.

It is thus clear that the paternalistic leadership can be closely related to patriarchy. This is a form of authoritarian style of leadership. This style of leadership is well respected in eastern nations such as China and India. In this style, the point of focus is the big community where the leader is responsible for all his (or her) group members. As said above if the leader creates an environment of loyalty through his or her behavior, this style can work wonders with the employees.

It is assumed that the leader in this style will always make the right decisions. It expects little to nothing from the employees.

It does not provide the employees with tools to grow. Thus, this style of leadership can hinder creativity and ultimately, the growth of the organization as well. Some people can think of it as an oppressive form of leadership.

Chapter Six: Leadership Behaviors and Development of Leadership Style and Skills

Character Strengths

Big Five personality factors

The Big Five Traits or the Five Factors is a personality model. It is one of the most popular and highly accepted models in the scientific world. It is not as popular as the Myers-Briggs model in laymen, but it is considered to be more serious and scientifically sound as compared to other models. It studies and analyzes different personalities and their behavior.

This model is known as the Big Five Model because according to this theory all human personalities can be divided into five, distinct and significant sections. These sections are known as dimensions. All of these sections are varied, distinct, unique, and independent of each other. This model is sometimes also known as the OCEAN model or the CANOE model as well. As the name suggests, these are the acronyms for the five dimensions.

According to this model of study, all people can be analyzed using some key factors present in their personality. These factors are responsible for our thoughts as well as behavior. However, personality traits cannot correctly understand a person's behavior in any given situation. The Big Five model then can help people to understand why people act in a certain way in certain situations. Thus, it is not a predictive method. It is not a typical model like other personality models such as the Type A/B personality model or the Myers and Briggs' model. The Big Five model is a 'traits' model.

Type models like the Myers and Briggs' are easy to remember and understand, but they are never scientifically sound. It is impossible to categorize people into simple and easy categories. The Big Five does not sort people into categories. It tries to differentiate people on the basis of their personalities and the traits that they display. Once this is done, the model puts people on a spectrum. A spectrum is far more flexible than regular categories.

It is now time to have a brief look at all the five dimensions as seen in the Big Five Model.

Openness

Openness is often thought to be a tendency to be open about feelings and thoughts. While this is true, in the Big Five Model, openness refers to the ability to take on new experiences, changes, plans, and ideas. Once upon a time this trait was also known as 'intellect', but to avoid unnecessary confusion it is now known as openness and 'intellect' has become obsolete.

A person who possess this trait can think in an abstract way. People who tend to have this trait are often creative, adventurous, and intellectual. These people love playing with ideas and thoughts. They are creative and try to seek new experiences. People who do not show this trait are often more focused, traditional, and practical. They avoid the unknown and off-beat paths. They try to stick to the traditions as much as possible.

Openness as a trait is related to the interconnections present in the regions of the brain. People who have Openness as their dominant trait tend to have more connections as compared to other people.

Conscientiousness

A person who is goal-oriented, persistent, and dedicated is supposed to have a dominant conscientiousness trait. People who have this trait as their dominant trait are often organized and determined. They concentrate on long-term goals and benefits and do not care about short term gratification. People who do not have this trait are often impulsive. They get sidetracked easily.

This trait is closely associated with the frontal lobe activity in the brain. The frontal lobe is considered as the 'executive' area of the brain as it controls, moderates, and regulates 'animal' and instinctual impulses. People who have this trait as their dominant trait tend to use the frontal part of their brain more than other people.

Extraversion

A person who loves the outside world and gets stimulation from it is supposed to have the 'Extraversion' trait. People with this trait try to seek attention from other people. They often like activities and situations where they can make new friends. They desire status, power, administration, and excitement. They are also highly romantically inclined. Compared to them, introverts try to save their energy. They do not care for social rewards.

Extraversion is related to dopamine. Dopamine a neurotransmitter that acts like a reward which keeps us motivated. People who have extraversion as their dominant trait tend to have a lot of dopamine.

Agreeableness

The people who tend to prioritize the needs and desires of other people over their own desires and requirements are said to display the 'agreeable' trait. People who are predominantly agreeable tend to be empathetic as well. They enjoy helping others and making them happy. People who do not display this trait often do not possess empathy. They are selfish and always put their problems in front of problems of others.

If this trait is dominant, then a lot of enhanced activity is seen in the superior temporal gyrus. This area of the brain is related to recognition of emotions and language processing.

Neuroticism

Some people tend to react negatively towards stimulants. They tend to show negative emotions such as guilt, sadness, fear, anxiety, and shame towards stimulants. These reactions can be classified as neuroticism.

This trait is often considered to be a warning sign. The people who tend to show these traits often think that there is something messed up with this world. Fear is supposed to be a reaction to danger, while guilt is a reaction to having done something wrong. But not all people have the same reaction in a moment. People who score a high on this level generally react to things in a negative manner. People who score a low score on this section tend to brush things off and move forward.

In the brain, neuroticism is related to many regions, including the regions that are responsible for processing negative stimuli, including aggressive dogs, angry faces, etc. It is also closely related to the regions that deal with negative emotions. According to a study, high neuroticism can also change the serotonin processing mechanism in the brain.

Big Five Traits and Personality

People are normally described as having low, high, or average levels of all the five traits Each of these factors is independent of other so it is possible that somebody can be highly extroverted by still low in If you want to understand an individual properly using the Big Five Model, it is first necessary to understand how they fair in each of the five dimensions. You can use a Big Five personality test (easily available online) to get a general understanding of your Big Five Traits.

History of the Big Five

The roots of the Big Five model can be traced back to a theory known as the lexical hypothesis. This theory believes that it is possible to create a taxonomy of individual difference by analyzing the language used by us to describe each other. Early researchers used various terms to describe personality traits, including "helpful," "friendly, "aggressive," and "creative." These researchers tried to organize these traits into various groups. For instance, people who were described as being friendly were also described as talkative, gregarious, and outgoing. Researchers soon realized that these trait adjectives often corresponded to the Big Five traits.

Nowadays, the Big Five model forms the basis of modern personality research. It is used to illustrate everything right from our personality, our personality factors, its relation with our income, etc.

Emotional Intelligence

Emotion is a wide range of behaviors, changes in the state of body and mind, and expressed feelings. Feelings, our likes, dislikes, and emotions all provide our lives meaning. They also cause us to be satisfied, happy, dissatisfied, or sad. Intelligence can be defined as the ability to use and gain knowledge and skills. If both of these are combined, we get Emotional Intelligence that can be defined as our ability to deal with other people efficiently. By understanding our own feelings, we can understand the feelings of others and evaluate them as well. There are five major elements of emotional intelligence. Let us have a look at them one by one.

Self-Awareness

This can be defined as our ability to recognize and analyze the motivations, moods, and abilities of ourselves. It also includes understanding the effects of the above three on others. If a person wants to become completely self-aware, he or she needs to learn how to monitor his or her emotional state. He or she should be able to identify his or her emotions, as well. Traits that make use emotionally mature include the ability to laugh at oneself, confidence, awareness, and perception.

Self-Regulation

This refers to the ability to control one's emotions and impulses. A good leader should think before he or she speaks or reacts. It is also related to the ability to express oneself in an appropriate manner.

If a person is emotionally mature in this category, he or she will always take responsibility for their action. He or she will be ready to adapt to changes and will always know how to respond appropriately to other people's emotions or irrational behavior.

Motivation

Motivation is closely related to a person's interest in self-improvement and learning. A person who is motivated will often be interested in learning things. A motivated person possesses the strength to keep on going forward even in the face of obstacles. Motivated people not only set goals, but they follow them. A person who is emotionally mature in this skill will have traits such as commitment and initiative. He or she will be committed towards the task and will tend to persevere even in the face of adversity.

Empathy

Empathy refers to the ability to understand other people's reactions and emotions. A person who is self-aware is often always empathetic. If you cannot understand yourself, you will rarely understand others. A person who is emotionally mature in this section will be interested in the problems of other people. He or she will have great anticipatory skills, especially in regard to people and their emotional responses towards situations. They also understand the social norms and the logic behind people's behavior.

Social Skills

This refers to the ability to pick up on sarcasm, jokes, puns, etc. It is also related to maintaining and managing friendship, friendly customer service, and finding common ground with others. If a person has emotional maturity in this skill, he or she will have good time management skills, good communication skills, and good leadership skills as well. He or she will be able to solve problems with ease and will be able to manage a large group of people effortlessly. He or she will possess excellent persuasion and negotiation skills.

Emotional intelligence plays a significant role in maintaining positive relationships with the people around them. This allows leaders to become successful leaders. Successful leaders are well known to be emotionally intelligent. They often have great relationships with the people they work with. Nowadays, organizations too tend to pick individuals for leadership positions who are in touch with their emotional side.

Leadership and Intelligence

Management experts have spent a lot of resources to find the connection between intelligence and leadership. That leadership and intelligence are compatible and correlated is a well-known fact.

The Connection between Leadership and Intelligence

Intelligent Leaders Listen and Learn

If you want to become a successful leader, you need to possess the qualities of listening to others and taking inputs from them. You should be able to listen and take inputs from everyone, including your subordinates as well. Intelligent leaders do not only care about plans but also know how to utilize others and get their help to plan activities. Leadership is a group activity and if you ever feel that your leadership is getting dangerously close to dictatorship, abort it.

Intelligence is essential as it allows leaders to evaluate other peoples' opinions and place them into the plans hypothetically. This way, leaders can check whether an idea can work in the plan or not. A great leader will always try to get valuable inputs from employees. This will not only help his or her plan, but it will also boost the confidence and morale of his or her employees.

A great leader understands the importance of communication. He or she should be able to communicate with his or her employees. Leaders need to talk and discuss their ideas with their employees. Employees can teach leaders a lot. Leaders need to adopt new strategies frequently. They can gain these strategies from their employees and team members.

Intelligent Leaders Plan Ahead

One of the major duties of leaders is planning and strategizing in the initial phases. A good leader will know how to adjust his or her plan according to situations and the obstacles. Damage control is essential for all organizations, but if the leader can anticipate impending problems, the damage can be prevented. Intelligent leaders are honest, and they will always let their team members know if there is something wrong or if things are not going according to the plan. Rumors spread quickly in difficult situations, and leaders should always be ready to comfort employees and help the situation to cool down.

Intelligent Leaders and Alliances

A team consists of many different people with varied personalities. Many times, not all team members like each other or are compatible with each other. They may have contrasting ideas or contradicting philosophies. This can lead to disastrous situations if not handled properly. A good leader can solve such problems and create strong bonds and firm alliances. Making different people work for the same goal while collaborating with each other is a sign of an intelligent and successful leader.

An intelligent leader can let his or her team members know how a goal can lead to mutual benefit and convince all the different individuals to work together. Team building and management are two essential skills that all leaders must possess.

Intelligent Leaders Respect

Only getting an MBA cannot help you become a top leader. You need to understand a lot of things and need to have a significant amount of people skills as well. Many top B-school graduates are smart, and this smartness sometimes instils a sense of superiority in them. They can be often boisterous and prideful. This often leads to problems. Experienced leaders are often stronger than smart but new leaders. It is thus necessary to respect the experience and learn as much as possible from them.

Intelligent Leaders Motivate

Intelligent leaders are often great leaders because they just do not get work done efficiently, but they also motivate their team members all the time. Motivation at the workplace is crucial, and a leader who can motivate team members is always a successful leader.

A leader should be able to understand the needs of his or her team members. He or she should also be able to understand what steps are necessary to motivate people. Each employee is a distinct individual with a distinct set of principles, values, and understandings. A leader cannot use the same method of motivation for each employee. He or she needs to analyze the employee and adjust the motivational method accordingly. Motivating the employees is essential, as they will keep the group alive and thriving.

These are some of the important connections between leadership and intelligence. It is clear from the above section that if a leader wants to be successful, he or she should possess various kinds of intelligence. A smart leader will always be a successful leader.

Self-efficacy for leadership

Efficacy is related to effectiveness and ability. It means the ability to produce the desired result. Thus, self-efficacy means a person's ability in any given situation. Self-efficacy is more about your own belief in your abilities than the true limit. What you believe about yourself has a significant impact on your psychology. It can control the way your brain engages with obstacles and stress.

Another plus point of self-efficacy is that people who have high amounts of it can achieve the given goals by performing the required tasks with ease. They are more likely to accomplish a goal as compared to other people. They are also more intuitive as compared to other people. Self-efficacy can help you avoid being a quitter. It can help you to be successful and bold.

Self-efficacy and Leadership

Nobody likes quitting, as it does not feel good at all. When we quit, we are usually left with insecurities, regret, and pain. We feel as if we have let ourselves down. These are some of the things that no one wants to feel ever. But self-efficacy can help you avoid these. As said earlier, your belief in yourself can help you become successful. So, if you want to become a great leader, you need to trust yourself and believe that you can lead people successfully. Possessing high self-efficacy can help you become a great leader. It affects your performance positively. It can also affect the performance of your group positively as well. Thus, self-efficacy can work wonders for leaders who want to be successful. You may be surprised to know, but as leaders, your perseverance, motivation, thoughts, vulnerabilities, wellbeing, and choices, all are dependent on your self-efficacy. Thus, almost every part of the leadership experience is closely controlled by self-efficacy.

People who have high self-efficacy tend to work better with challenges and problems. If they ever experience a pushback, they can encounter it with calmness. They possess immense self-control and can act with a lot of precision in stressful and difficult situations. They are often willing to put in a lot of efforts to lead the group. They take care of the group's needs.

Leadership Self-Efficacy for Direction Setting

A leader is supposed to plan and guide his or her team towards the goal. If a leader does not possess good directional and guidance skills, he or she can never be a great leader. Self-efficacy can help you become a great director or guide, as it will enable you to be confident about your ability to guide. It will encourage you all the time. It will also boost your confidence regarding problem-solving and other related objectives. Your self-beliefs in this area are often related to your past successes or even failures. They are also closely associated with your beliefs about your intelligence.

Leadership Self-Efficacy for Overcoming Obstacles

One of the major jobs that a leader is supposed to do is overcoming obstacles. The world is constantly changing, and if a leader wants to move with the world, he or she needs to move quickly. A leader needs to learn how to overcome limitations. These limitations can be varied in nature. For instance, a leader may have to face personal limitations, social limitations, individual limitations, etc. A leader needs to possess specific skills to overcome obstacles without harming his or her team. Some skills that are necessary to overcome obstacles include serving others, the ability to pivot, overseeing work, and building momentum. Some other things that are necessary to be a successful taskmaster include drive, self-control, and being action-oriented. A person who is self-motivated and is flexible will always be a great problem solver.

Leadership Self-Efficacy for Gaining Commitment

Achieving commitment is crucial for leadership. You need to have the support of your team if you want to succeed. If no one is committed to your cause, you will not have a team and thus have no one to lead. Gaining commitment comes naturally to some, but for others, it can be incredibly difficult. This is because commitment relies heavily on interpersonal skills. If you possess excellent interpersonal skills, you can easily get others to commit to your cause, but if you lack these skills, it will be quite a task to talk and convince other people. Interpersonal skills are not related to communication skills only; they are also related to your social skills. If you can relate to others with ease and can guide them as well, then you possess decent to good interpersonal skills. Your trustworthiness and clarity of conversation can also make you a great communicator.

All of the above-mentioned skills can be developed with practice and dedication. Treat each conversation or interaction as a practice ground to practice these skills. Soon you will be able to notice a difference in your skills. It is necessary to become a people-person if you want to succeed in the modern world.

Self-awareness for your insecurities is a great way to work through them. It is necessary to reflect upon your ideas and thoughts and insecurities. This will allow you to tackle them effectively. Tackling insecurities is difficult, and it needs a lot of dedication and passion. It is impossible to do it without a lot of self-efficacy.

Thus, it is clear that self-efficacy is necessary for almost all aspects of leadership, and it can really help you become a great leader.

Self-monitoring

Self-monitoring as a concept was first explained by Mark Snyder in 1970s. It is used to analyze how people monitor themselves and how they monitor their behaviors, expressions, self-presentations, and non-verbal communication as well. Each individual has a different capacity of expression and showing their emotions. Some people are great at controlling their emotions and expressions, while some like to wear their mind on their sleeve. Self-monitoring is a personality trait that is useful for regulating your behavior according to the social setting.

People who are concerned with their expression in self-presentation often tend to monitor their audience. Self-monitors try to understand how groups and individuals will react to them. They also pay close attention to how the group or the individual will perceive them. Some personality types act spontaneously, while others tend to control their emotions and expressions purposefully. These people adjust their behavior according to the social situation.

Snyder's self-monitoring scale came into existence in the year 1974. It is used to measure whether an individual has the ability to change their image using impression management in different social interactions and settings. The score is calculated after a small quiz of 25 questions. The test taker is asked to answer the questions according to his or her ideas and thought process. It is used to determine how an individual may use non-verbal signs. It is also used to understand how a particular individual may react in particular situations. The questions are generally True or False type questions.

Low self-monitors

Low self-monitors generally display expressive controls that are concrete. They rarely change their ideas, beliefs, attitudes, and tend to maintain the same disposition in every situation. They never change, regardless of social circumstance. These people often do not care about social context and situations. They believe that displaying an image that is not congruent with their inner-self is fake and should not be done. People who self-monitor often adjust their behavior according to the situation but people who refuse to adjust themselves are often uncompromising, angry, aggressive, and insistent. This is why they are often condemned and disliked. This often leads to the generation of feelings such as isolation, anxiety, anger, guilt, depression, and low self-esteem.

These people are often indiscreet, which makes social situations awkward and uncomfortable. It can often lead to the loss of clients, friends, family, colleague, and in some cases, a career as well. People who are willing to adjust their behavior often find situations easy. People find self-monitors pleasant, receptive, and benevolent.

High self-monitors

People who monitor themselves closely are often known as high self-monitors. They often act in certain ways. They are often highly responsive to situational context and social cues. High self-monitors are often thought of as social pragmatists who can build images to impress others and gain positive feedback. Compared to low self-monitors, high self-monitors often display more expressive control. They are also concerned about the appropriateness of the situation. These people are always ready to adjust their behavior for their own benefits. They are often thought to be pleasant, more receptive, and benevolent, and people react to them in a positive manner as well.

Barriers

Leadership differences affected by gender

A lot of research has been done whether sex differences in leadership exists or not. Similarly, a lot of research has been conducted on whether the differences exist, and whether they exist on relationship levels or task-based levels. Leadership is an intricate process in which individuals guides his or her group towards a goal. According to certain studies, it was found that there exists some sort of difference between the leadership style and methodology of the genders. For instance, women use a more participative style of leadership as compared to men. But there are also certain studies that say that there exists no difference between the genders.

Until recently, almost all leadership positions were held by men and thus men were considered to be more effective leaders. Women rarely got the chance to be leaders leading major corporations and groups, and thus the data regarding their behavior was lacking. But the trend is changing now, and women have become prevalent in the corporate world, enjoying topmost positions as well. Thus, the gender gap is reducing, and the stereotypes associated with leadership are changing as well. But then there are strong proofs that say that the gender gap still exists.

For instance, while women display a lot of effective leadership qualities in some studies, men are still stereotypically considered to be better leaders than women.

There exist a lot of stereotypes regarding the differences between female and male leaders, along with a variety of research and personal anecdotes as well. While there exists a lot of correlation between the accounts and observations, it also reveals a lot of biases. It is possible that these stereotypes are subjective and are perhaps clouded by preconceived notions.

According to preconceived notions and stereotypes, male managers follow a top-down style of leadership. They are also supposed to be hierarchical. On the other hand, female leaders are more egalitarian. They are more supportive and helpful as well. But these are gross stereotypes and generalities. They cannot portray the cultural and individual differences.

Difference Between Male Leader and Female Leaders

Collaboration and Individualism

As per research, female leaders tend to appreciate groups and team efforts more than other leaders. They are more collaborative and try to combine the skills and knowledge of all the team members. Male leaders are supposed to be more individualistic. They create a work atmosphere where people compete with each other because they believe that competition leads to growth.

Egalitarianism and hierarchy

Female bosses praise people for their achievements. Under female bosses' voices are heard and they are valued too. Male bosses focus more on experience, skills, and knowledge. The 'female' approach works great for the morale of the employees while the 'male' approach can help you achieve more predictable results.

Transformational Work and Transactional Work

Female leaders, as said earlier are supposed to be more helpful and supportive. They try to build and develop the skills of their employees and groom them to take up more responsibilities. On the other hand, male bosses use the transactional method of leadership. In this method a person a rewarded whenever they complete a task successfully. Female leaders show a more transformational form of leadership which is good for employees as it leads to continuous learning. The transactional, method, however, is great if you want to get things done quickly.

Perception vs Reality

Women leaders are often described as more compassionate, and this compassion is considered to be a positive trait in female leadership. 'Analytical' is often used to describe a male leadership style. Both analytical and compassionate are subjective terms, and thus, their meanings can differ significantly. It is better to look at leadership styles in a more objective way.

Individual vs. General Traits

Leadership is a subjective term, and it is highly individualistic as well. There is a lot of difference between the leadership styles of individuals. Similarly, there exist a lot of differences between the leadership styles of some men and women. For instance, some men may display stereotypically female leadership traits such as collaboration and compassion, while women may display male traits such as authoritarianism and competitive.

It can be said that a large number of women leaders display a leadership style that is stereotypically associated with men as the hierarchical aspects of the workforce all genders to indulge into specific practices that help them to reach the top.

Non-western

Many people in the West still use the Western models of leadership, but now people have realized that this method is not sufficient in the times of globalization. This is why many organizations nowadays try to accommodate cultural differences and are trying to incorporate different approaches to leadership. It has now become crucial for managers to learn how to adapt to their surroundings and circumstances.

Leading employees from different cultural backgrounds have become an everyday challenge for a lot of leaders. Cultural differences and how they work in-group as well as personal relationships have now become especially crucial.

Local cultures can significantly change the definition, as well as the application of leadership methods.

It is important to understand the historical development of the traditions in different nations.

For leaders who are supposed to manage global teams, it is recommended to get acquainted with the cultures of the members. It will allow you to understand their behavior and what sort of leadership will work the best with them. If leaders go the extra mile in the beginning, they will not have to face any other significant problems in the future. It is necessary to get acquainted with the local environment and cultural aspects as well. However, avoid going 'native'. This will make you seem less authentic, and people will think that you are trying to appropriate their culture. It is recommended to avoid the behavior of the locals. Instead of doing this, try to understand the cultural practices and act as authentic as possible.

Chapter 7 How Great Leaders Inspire Action/ The 7 Great Leadership Traits

The Mandate of Heaven

The "Mandate of Heaven" is an ancient philosophical concept that originated in China in the Zhou Dynasty around the year (1046-256 BCE) According to the Mandate, the Emperor of China was supposed to be virtuous enough to rule. If the Emperor were not able to fulfill the obligations of the emperor, then he would lose the Mandate and thus the right to be the Emperor.

Construction of Mandate

The Mandate was constructed using the following four principles:

1. Heaven gives the Emperor the right to rule.
2. As there exists only one Heaven, so there can be only one Emperor
3. The Emperor's virtues make him capable of ruling.
4. None of the dynasties can rule permanently.

There are various examples when the Emperor lost the Mandate of Heaven due to reasons such as invasions, peasant uprisings, famine, droughts, earthquakes, and floods. Floods and droughts both lead to famines that ultimately lead to peasant uprisings. Thus, most of the above reasons were interconnected.

Although the Mandate of Heaven sounds sort of similar to the concept of the 'Divine Right of Kings' in Europe, it operated in a much different way. In the European model, a particular family was granted the right to rule by God. The Right would never change even if the ruler's behavior were seen to be preposterous. This is why we have many examples of incompetent and insane European rulers. According to the Divine Right, no one could oppose the king, as it was a sin.

The Mandate of Heaven, however, justified rebellion against incompetent, tyrannical, or unjust rulers. If the rebellion was successful in overthrowing the ruler, then the Mandate was lost, and the leader of the rebels had gained it. The Mandate of Heaven was not hereditary like the Diving Right of Kings. It did not even care about royalty or royal birth. Anyone could become a Kind if they had the approval of Heaven.

The Mandate of Heaven in Action

The Mandate of Heaven was used to justify the overthrow of the Shang Dynasty by the Zhou Dynasty. Zhou leaders believed that the Shang emperors had become unfit of ruling because of rampant corruption.

After some years the Zhou dynasty crumbled but as there existed no opposition leader, a sort of Civil war begun in China. Ultimately the Qin Dynasty gained the Mandate but lost it soon. It was then gained by the Han Dynasty. This continued until the end of the Qing Dynasty in 1911.

Effects of the Idea

The Mandate of Heaven was considered to be highly important in China and neighboring countries, including Korea and Annam. As the rulers were afraid of losing the Mandate, they often carried out their duties in an honorary manner.

The Mandate also allowed social mobility, as even a peasant could become the emperor. It also gave a scapegoat for inexplicable events such as famines, droughts, floods, etc.

Machiavelli

A great and successful Machiavellian leader should possess five important traits. These traits decide whether a leader will be successful or not. These characteristics will be explained in detail below.

Fear

In medieval times, leaders believed that if their subjects were scared of them, they would not revolt. In today's society, this equation has changed significantly. For instance, nowadays, Presidents desire to love more than fear. This is especially true about democratic nations. If you decide that you want to be feared, it is necessary that your subjects should not hate you. There is a difference between hatred and fear. If people hate you, they will surely make schemes against you.

Support of the Governed

The second important trait that a successful leader must possess is the support of people. Without support, a leader cannot perform any actions. Machiavelli stresses the importance of people supporting the leader on almost every page of his book. Machiavelli believes that it is necessary for the leader to have support from the people because no military exercise can be successful without mercenary units. This means that you cannot expand your territory if you do not have people supporting you. You need to satisfy the basic needs of your people, or they will not support you.

Virtue

According to Machiavelli, a leader should either have virtue or should at least pretend to be virtuous. A virtuous leader can easily gain the support of people. It becomes easy for him or her to be in power for a long time. Machiavelli also says that having good virtues can hinder your rule, as it will limit your power significantly. For this Machiavelli suggests that the ruler should be virtuous in public and should do whatever is necessary to continue his rule in private.

Arms

Machiavelli believed that it is better to use your own forces instead of using mercenaries and other forces. Hiring soldiers can lead to a lot of negative results. If you hire your own people to fight for you, they will stay true to the cause until their last breath. Hired soldiers may flee when the times get tough. Auxiliary units are particularly bad because they will not be ready to die for you. This will make your army weak.

Intelligence

Intelligence is essential if you want to be a good leader. According to Machiavelli, intelligence is the most important trait that a successful leader must-have. Without intelligence, a King cannot rule and control people. He cannot gain the support of the people either. Intelligence helps the king to rule his territory with complete confidence. A King who depends on the decisions of his minister or assistant can be easily manipulated. It is always better to be smart and wise.

Napoleon

Napoleon is considered one of the greatest conquerors and leaders in the history of the modern world. Napoleon rose around the time of the French Revolution and changed French history forever.

During the peak of his reign, Napoleon controlled almost the whole of Europe. He was able to do so with the help of ambition, ingenuity, and cold-bloodedness.

History

Napoleon was born on the island of Corsica on 15 August 1769. When he was young, he was highly interested in warfare. Unsurprisingly, he went to a military college and studied warfare and became the 2nd Lieutenant in the artillery division.

France was going through a crisis around this time, which was soon followed by the French Revolution. Napoleon saw this and soon commanded the forces against tyranny and the British. He became a brigadier general at a young age.

Napoleon was ambitious right from his childhood, and thus he soon started attacking neighboring nations such as Russia, Italy, Austria, and Great Britain. Soon, he was captured almost the whole continent of Europe. But he was not able to conquer Russia or Great Britain. He suffered a heavy defeat in Moscow that was soon followed by a massive and career-ending defeat in the battle of Waterloo.

He was later exiled and passed away by stomach cancer on 5 May 1821. Some people believe that he was poisoned.

Leadership Lessons

Vision and Imagination

Napoleon is still praised for his exemplary vision and imagination. When he was the Emperor, he would win over men by showing how visionary he was. He would come up with various military tactics that were often way ahead of any other leaders of his time.

Thus, having a great vision is essential if you want to be a successful leader. A leader needs to know where he is leading his people. It is also recommended to share your vision with your employees as it will encourage and inspire them.

Know your folks

Napoleon understood that gaining the support of people was crucial. He would go around and know each of his soldiers by his name. This allowed him to establish personal contact with them.

People love to control the whole organization by sitting behind a table and directing orders through phone calls and emails. But organizations are often organic where you need to form bonds and connections if you want to be successful. Organizations are built upon relationships and establishing new and maintaining old relationships will make your organization grow. Take some time and get to know your team. Learn things about them and impress them.

Persistence is essential

If you want to be successful and victorious, you need to be persistent. You cannot achieve success if you are not dedicated and passionate about something. For instance, Napoleon was exiled, but he came back to take the throne of France.

Being consistent in your efforts will always help you to succeed. It is true that you may fail a couple of times in the beginning, but with time, dedication, and persistent, you will rise again and ultimately succeed.

Sun Tzu

In his seminal work The Art of War, Sun Tsu put forward the theory of leadership. According to him, a leader should possess five important traits. Let us have a look at these five traits, one by one.

Intelligence

If leaders want to succeed, they should be competent in every aspect of their work. They must exceed their own expectations if they want to become a great leader. They need to understand the needs of their colleagues. They need to understand their position in the organization as compared to the competitors. Leaders should understand how to take care of their intelligence. Boisterous leaders often fail.

Credibility

According to Sun Tzu, credibility is crucial if you want to be a great leader. Credibility comes from competence and trustworthiness. A leader should be able to display his experience, knowledge, and prowess.

Humaneness

Leaders should always be respectful of everyone. This includes everyone right from peers, subordinates, and even competitors. Great leaders understand that being humble will help them achieve great success. Humaneness is essential between leaders as well.

Leaders need to learn how to look at people as individuals and not just a team.

Courage

For Sun Tzu, a great leader is always courageous. He should be decisive and bold. The leader who bucks down due to pressure is not a great leader. Their judgment and prowess will be questioned by their peers and subordinates both. Courage enables leaders to take risks and find potential opportunities. Confidence and boldness provide a sense of credibility to his or her actions.

Discipline

According to Sun Tzu, a great leader is not only well trained, but he or she is also highly disciplined.

According to him, a leader should be ready all the time to fight in a battle. Leaders should evaluate situations and should never make rash decisions. This is often covered in their training. Discipline is learned and enforced through a complex and continuous system of punishments and rewards. Ultimately, for Sun Tzu, a leader needs to be bold and smart.

Conclusion

Thank you for buying this book! I hope you found it informative and interesting.

It is clear that leadership is one of the most crucial aspects of today's world. Today's world is highly focused on change and competition and to survive in this world, you need to adapt to change to quickly and be competitive as well. You also need to versatile, dedicated, and bold if you want to be a successful leader. Without this, no one can survive the trepidation of the modern corporate world. To become a great leader, you need to possess several qualities, all of which are related closely related to passion and strength of character. You cannot become a successful leader if you do not understand the contemporary world.

This book is a great guidebook that can help you become a great leader. It consists of various in-depth chapters that will help you become a successful leader. It opens with a chapter dealing with myths associated with leadership so that you can enter the world of development without any preconceived notions. An in-depth chapter dealing with different styles of leadership is one of the fortes of this book. It will allow you to understand which kind of leadership style you use and whether it is suitable for your workplace or not. It will also help you to make the necessary changes in your leadership style and adapt it according to your team. A chapter on various tips, tricks, and methods will help you to hone your leadership style and will make you a skillful leader. It will teach you how negativity and fear are two of the biggest enemies of a good leader. Some sections related to the barriers in leadership style and great historical leaders and their leadership style would help you understand what to do and what not to do while traversing the corporate world.

This book has covered almost everything that a leader needs to know to become a successful leader. In-depth chapters, well-researched topics, good examples, etc. all make this book one of the best leadership guides in the market. What makes it especially suitable for beginners is that it is written in a simple and lucid manner avoiding the complex jargon of the contemporary world. But this does not mean that it is not suitable for experts. The level of knowledge and information combined in this book will offer something to every reader-beginner or expert both.

While this book can help you become a great leader, it cannot work on its own. The clear message of this book is that if you want to be a great leader, you need to be dedicated and strong, and this book will help you to become so.

If you enjoyed this book and found some benefit in reading this, I'd like to hear from you and hope that you could take some time to post a review. Your feedback and support will help this author to greatly improve his writing craft for future projects and make this book even better.

Please keep in touch with me or for questions and advice: wswainpublishing@gmail.com

Thank you and good luck!

Peter Allen

References

http://blog.vernalmgmt.com/the-myth-of-innate-leadership/

https://www.forbes.com/sites/ekaterinawalter/2013/10/08/5-myths-of-leadership/#52872afe314e

https://www.thebalancecareers.com/common-myths-about-leadership-2275821

https://www.inc.com/mithu-storoni/these-5-rules-can-protect-your-team-from-toxic-negativity.html

https://yscouts.com/10-narcissistic-leadership-characteristics/

https://tomflick.com/2015/12/02/fear-vs-respect-why-leading-through-fear-is-never-the-answer/

https://www.psychologicalscience.org/news/minds-business/dominant-leaders-are-bad-for-groups.html

https://sites.psu.edu/leadership/2017/04/09/15415/

https://www.lollydaskal.com/leadership/7-powerful-habits-that-make-you-more-assertive/

https://www.forbes.com/sites/glennllopis/2013/05/20/6-effective-ways-listening-can-make-you-a-better-leader/#5af0213e1756

https://trainingindustry.com/blog/leadership/5-important-communication-skills-for-leaders/

https://www.fastcompany.com/3054067/7-habits-of-leaders-who-inspire-loyalty

https://www.n2growth.com/ceos-feared-or-respected/

https://www.businessinsider.com/how-to-be-a-leader-people-want-to-follow-2014-10?IR=T

https://hbr.org/2004/09/why-people-follow-the-leader-the-power-of-transference

https://www.thebalancecareers.com/developing-your-employees-2275869

https://studiousguy.com/paternalistic-leadership-style-types-examples/

https://www.eskill.com/blog/task-people-oriented-management/

https://www.verywellmind.com/what-is-democratic-leadership-2795315

https://www.verywellmind.com/what-is-laissez-faire-leadership-2795316

https://www.verywellmind.com/what-is-autocratic-leadership-2795314

http://www.leadershipexpert.co.uk/leadership-family.html

http://fltiofcolorado.colostate.edu/what-is-flti/what-is-family-leadership/

https://community.mbaworld.com/blog/b/weblog/posts/the-importance-of-self-leadership

https://www.brighthubpm.com/resource-management/93165-group-leadership-skills/

https://iedunote.com/management

http://www.yourarticlelibrary.com/organization/organization-meaning-definition-concepts-and-characteristics/53217

https://www.csoonline.com/article/2137088/the-anatomy-of-leadership---a-sun-tzu-perspective.html

http://www.leadershipgeeks.com/napoleon-leadership/

https://soapboxie.com/social-issues/Characteristics-of-a-Machiavellian-Leader

https://www.thoughtco.com/the-mandate-of-heaven-195113

https://www.ideasforleaders.com/ideas/leadership-beyond-the-western-model

https://en.wikipedia.org/wiki/Sex_differences_in_leadership

https://en.wikipedia.org/wiki/Self-monitoring

https://jenniferspoelma.com/blog-feed/what-is-self-efficacy-and-how-does-it-relate-to-leadership

https://aboutleaders.com/leadership-and-intelligence/#gs.m8qcln

http://theimportanceofemotionalintelligence.weebly.com/the-5-components.html

https://www.truity.com/book/big-five-personality-model

https://www.entrepreneur.com/article/312552

https://bizfluent.com/about-5445316-difference-between-male-female-leadership.html

Printed in Great Britain
by Amazon

44539265R00076